POWER
AND SEXUALITY

POWER

AND

SEXUALITY

The Emergence of Canon Law at the Synod of Elvira

SAMUEL LAEUCHLI

Temple University Press

Philadelphia

Temple University Press, Philadelphia 19122
© 1972 by Temple University. All rights reserved
Published 1972
Printed in the United States of America

International Standard Book Number: 0–87722–015–8
Library of Congress Catalog Card Number: 72–83671

To Cyril C. Richardson

CONTENTS

PREFACE

When I came to Temple University four years ago, and joined the newly established department of religion, I was excited by the chance it gave me to seek out and test new methodological approaches to the ancient church. This study on the Council of Elvira is an experiment in methodology, which arose out of my graduate patristic seminars and out of discussion with colleagues in other disciplines. I am grateful to many Temple University people, above all to Violet Ketels of the English Department, who untangled my language problems and made many valuable suggestions, and to T. P. Burke who was always willing to debate problems of theology and history. A group of graduate students, David Efroymson, James Biechler, Jerome McBride, George Sherman, and John White, worked with me to prepare the new English translation of the canons—the appendix of this volume.

POWER
AND SEXUALITY

One

LANGUAGE AND EVENT

In the year A.D. 309, a number of bishops and presbyters travelled over the Roman roads of southern Spain, assembled in a basilica of what is today the shining Andalusian town of Granada and in eighty-one canonic decisions asserted their authority over their churches. These canons, the first of their kind to have survived in the history of Christianity, are a fascinating witness to the evolution of the ancient church. They are full of dramatic interpersonal confrontations, of tensions between language and event, of the contradictions in Christian moral demands, and they are portentous of the sweeping religious success of the church. By identifying the canons' various linguistic patterns, frequently at odds with each other, and by exposing the conditions and tensions producing these patterns, I shall be able to examine the currents and crosscurrents operating during the council; by analyzing the equivocations in the canons, I mean to demonstrate the dynamic of ancient Christianity at the moment of its crucial transformation from a sectarian to an imperial religion.

Scholars have been analyzing these canons for years. Employing the vast information available about the ancient church and classical civilization, they have related the canons to their context of the Constantinian age, they have compared this synod with subsequent assemblies of the fourth century, and they have studied the various aspects of the council's legal language. There exist studies on the *flamines,* the priests of the imperial religion, on Ossius of Cordoba, who played a key role in the council, on the problem of iconoclasm which is the concern of can. 36, and on the famous demand for clerical continence in can. 33. This extensive research on Elvira and the Constantinian age is the basis of this work.[1]

However, scholarship which examines the texts in relation to earlier, contemporary, and subsequent texts, treating them as if they were explicit renderings of what the church believed and enacted at the time, does not suffice, no matter how minutely it is done. It fails to offer meaningful explanations for many of the extraordinary inconsistencies in what seem to be naive and simple canonic decisions, and it fails to satisfy our doubts whether all of the constantly reiterated threats in them were actually carried out. The failure is due to a basic misunderstanding as to what such texts represent. Time and again, they have been treated as abstract legal statements with a given, static meaning. What if they were not static legal formulations, but end products of violent group clashes, the last verbalized stage in a series of events, namely the conciliar debates, and behind them the tumultuous history of Iberian Christianity? The texts, on first reading, seem to imply that the bishops meted out all punishments by the book. But what if the penalties were sometimes only threats used as defensive tactics and weapons in bitter church struggles?

There are many indications in these canons that they were not products of cool reflection and of harmonious teamwork among bishops kindred in mind. When a number of canons speak to the same problem, they do not necessarily reflect a monolithic opinion or a balanced evaluation of a difficult legal problem; rather, they contain evidences of group confrontations. Actually, the canons imply a sequence of encounters; they reveal fears, desires, shifting stances, and fixed positions among those who made the decisions; they record a process, not merely a result; they uncover, upon close inspection, a

1. C. J. Hefele and H. Leclercq, *Histoire des Conciles,* vol. 1 (Paris, 1907), pp. 212–64; Pius Gams, *Kirchengeschichte von Spanien,* vol. 2 (Regensburg, 1864), pp. 1–136; the best monograph is still A. W. W. Dale, *The Synod of Elvira and Christian Life in the Fourth Century* (London, 1882), misunderstood, and attacked by V. C. de Clercq in his *Ossius of Cordova* (Washington, D.C., 1954), pp. 87–147. J. Gaudemet, "Elvire" in *Dict. d'Hist. et de Géogr. Eccl.* 15:312–48 and H. Leclercq, "Elvira" in *Dict. d'Arch. Chrét. et de Lit.* 4:2687–94.

collision occurring at that moment in ancient Christianity. The arbitrariness and the discrepancies in ethical values which occur are understandable if the canons are seen as the result of such human clashes.[2]

It does not suffice to interpret canonical texts as if they meant what they seem to say on first reading and as if they were direct, rational statements of what their authors intended and of what actually happened. Patristic research must free itself from what I am tempted to call "historical docetism"—the temptation to ignore the agony and the ambiguity, hopeful and tragic at once, in the human personality and hence in the human word. Just as there had been in the ancient church a christological docetism which tried by various devices to extract the divine, the "kernel," the authentic and unchangeable, from the body, from the shell, from the contextual and changeable, so there exists still a historical docetism which refuses to take into account the fact that language, though it sometimes means what it seems to say on first reading, sometimes does not; that the meaning of a text does not come from the abstract content of that text, but from the human encounter in the event which produced the text; and that when language is alive it has the quality of ambiguity. "Each word is true and false, that is the nature of the word," says Max Frisch's Stiller, the man who "has no language for reality."[3] The historian must search, therefore, for a methodology which reckons with the contextual and equivocal character of the text and attempts to understand the dynamic of the events which produced that text. The task is to recreate the past event as concretely as possible in order to get a better understanding of the text. Such methodology will have to take seriously that a believer of the church may at times mean the opposite of what he expresses and that the language of the past not only reveals the Christian's belief, but also conceals it. The tensions

---

2. Dale (p. 89) states that the task of the council was to "create a uniform system of discipline." I distinguish the attempt to create discipline from the results of that attempt.

3. Max Frisch, *Stiller* (Frankfurt, 1965), pp. 65, 133.

and collisions responsible for such ambiguities are frequently indications of major historical mutations.

We can illustrate the tension between express and hidden meanings of synodal texts, and the relation between the text and the personal and social dynamics of the synod by a comparison of three canons. Can. 13 condemns virgins who, after having dedicated their lives to God, committed some kind of sexual transgression, or *moechia*. The first part of the canon—I shall call it 13a—consists of a condemnation of them: "Virgins who have consecrated themselves to God, if they break their vow of virginity and turn to lust instead, not realizing what they lose, shall not be given communion at the end." The second part, 13b, qualifies the radical condemnation just pronounced by offering mercy, under cautiously phrased conditions, to some of these poor creatures: "If, however, corrupted by the fall of their weak body only once, they do penance for the rest of their lives, and abstain from intercourse so that they only seem fallen, they may receive communion at the end." This canon contains an exceedingly strict condemnation in the first part, but offers a curious, almost contradictory reason (if they fall only once, they only seem fallen) as a qualification in the second part.

Can. 18, likewise, offers a condemnation for sexual transgression, not on the part of virgins, but of clerics: "Bishops, presbyters, and deacons, if—once placed in the ministry—they are discovered to be sexual offenders, shall not receive communion, not even at the end, because of the scandal and the heinousness of their crime." Exactly as in can. 13, this canon has a strict anathema: We shall not forgive you such a sin. But it does not contain a second qualifying part; it allows for no exception. While some of the girls condemned in can. 13 were given a chance of mercy, *in finem,* the clerics in can. 18 were not.

In can. 19, as in the preceding one, bishops, presbyters, and deacons are addressed: "Bishops, presbyters and deacons are not to abandon their territories for commercial reasons, nor should they run around the provinces seeking after profitable business; in order to procure their livelihood, let them rather send a son or freedman, an employee, a friend, or whomever they want; if they want to pursue business, let them do it within their own province." This decision chides the clergy for monetary activities, but it does not pronounce any condemnation. The crucial formula of 13 and 18, *nec in finem,* does not appear in can. 19. What happened if a cleric did not comply? The language of the canon is rather uncertain: if the clerics do not want to comply, let them do business at least only in their own provinces. What would happen if they did not hold even to that rule? The canon does not commit itself.

These three canons contain three different modes of punishment or prohibition. The first is a two-part distinction between strictest anathema and exception, the second contains only anathema, and the third contains only prohibition without the strict anathema. The differences among these canons lead us to raise some pertinent questions about the synod which passed these decisions:

Why did the synod give an exception to the women, but not to their own peers, other clerics, in matters of sexual transgression?

Why did the synod treat bishops differently in matters of sexuality and in matters of economics?

Was the relationship between the clerics of the synod and women different from their relationship with men?

Was a struggle going on, and are these three canons evidences of that struggle? Does that mean that different groups won in can. 13 from those who won in can. 19, for instance?

Does the two-part decision of can. 13 mean that the synod were not as sure as they sounded, and therefore added 13b to 13a? Were they sure in can. 18 since they did not add a qualification in the latter?

Or is the opposite true? Was can. 18 phrased so as to express the one-upmanship of the majority over a minority, but also the recognition that it was too dangerous to take advantage of the "victory"?

Did the synod in can. 13 combine harshness with leniency because they felt repressed and guilty? Did they deliver their anathema (13a) out of anger at repression, but were they nevertheless so stirred by guilty memories of their own sexuality, be it fantasy or act, that they were swayed to leniency?

Did this mixture of repression and guilt not operate in can. 18, and does the difference between one canon's being addressed to women and the other's to men explain the disparity in punishment?

Did can. 19 not contain any real penalty because in economic matters it was totally unfeasible to enforce the group code of the church, while in sexual matters it seemed more possible?

These questions make us suspect that in and behind the differences among canonic decisions an exciting human drama took place. In their syntactical rhythm the canons sound certain, but their discrepancies betray the council's uncertainty. It is the purpose of this book to present a methodology by which evidences and hints of the drama, of the Christian clergy's quest for power, can be isolated and identified, thereby uncovering the process that led to this drama. Working with the patterns abstracted from the canonic language, one discovers that the legal-communal dimension, so often read literally, is ambiguous and that operative in it is a personal dimension of equal ambiguity. A canon is by no means a timeless essence, but a statement of situational responses. This analysis succeeds if it enables the reader to grasp the extraordinary complexity that characterizes the very beginning of ecclesiastical canonic law.

With all its hidden and open dynamic, the canon was an action concretized; it was historical evolution in process. To be sure, there were innumerable actions and events behind these canons—in Roman Spain, in Spanish Christianity, in Christian Baetica—before and during that synod of Elvira. Yet that synodal event was crucial. The words which were fused out of the crucible of the meeting were the reflections and partial expressions of the action going on there. That action contained both control and search, certainty and experiment. In the canons the clerics exerted their leadership over their people, offering them a set of redemptive values and a safe social framework in which believers could feel at home; but they also acted by facing each other, and through that confrontation they sought to control both their peers and their churches. They attempted to channel Spanish Christianity into certain directions, and they searched for solutions. Their need to control their churches stimulated them to search out a way to go. Not all such control and search, however, had the same weight. The canons of Elvira consist of a sequence of multiple actions with multiple implications.

Here, then, begins the challenge to historical inquiry. The event is gone. The bishops and presbyters are long gone from the fertile plain of Granada with the snow-capped Sierra Nevada on the horizon. Much of what happened at Elvira is, of course, irretrievable. The events of our own age are veiled and hard for us to understand. The relationship between contemporary language and life is not deciphered easily. How much more enigmatic, then, seem the issues of sixteen hundred years ago. Furthermore, we possess no letters, no minutes, no interviews illuminating the personalities or procedures of the council. If we had something like secretarial notes, we would at least have some guidelines to the inner workings of the event. Of the men involved, only Ossius, the famous bishop of Cordoba, is known beyond the council. The city of Granada contains practically no Roman traces. The odds against reconstructing the synod of Elvira by primary documentation are indeed overwhelming.

Yet we are not left in the dark. In the canons that have survived, the observer discovers traces of a human drama in the inferable procedures and patterns of group confrontations. In the first place, we have evidence that the canons represent the final verbal expressions of the results of a communal encounter. The synods of the ancient church were dynamic group processes.[4] This study will show that the canons can not have resulted from the deliberations of a homogeneous group applying a set of consistent criteria; neither can they have been the product of an individual single-handedly ruling on

4. Eduard Schwartz, "Die Kanonessammlungen der alten Reichskirche," *Gesammelte Schriften,* vol. 4 (Berlin, 1960), pp. 159ff.; Hamilton Hess, *The Canons of the Council of Sardica* (Oxford, 1958), pp. 26ff.

matters of the church. In their enigmatic variations the canons reflect a complex group process behind the decisions.

The nature of the decision-making process at the synod of Elvira can be deduced from secular antique parallels. The relationship between Christian councils and crucial meetings of ancient Rome has been demonstrated clearly.[5] When the Senate met, one of its members presented a case: the *relatio*. There followed proposed decisions, *sententiae,* again from members of the assembly, possibly with amendments. There might be a debate, *altercatio,* over several sententiae, from among which the majority vote emerged. This final vote took place probably in the form of an acclamation. What resulted was a curial decision, at one time called *senatus consultum*.[6] To be sure, one can not be certain that the procedure occurred precisely in this form in every province and in every secular or religious assembly. But just as the documents of the Synod of Sardica make it clear how much the Christian church followed pagan procedures, so the canons of Elvira begin with the official Roman *placuit,*[7] with the synod behaving thereby like a Roman legislative body. This analysis will present one piece of evidence after another which demonstrate that the clerics deciding the conflicts in Spanish Christianity acted as an urban or provincial assembly: they made decisions as municipal leaders, they controlled the behavior patterns of their subordinates, they played with mercy and wrath in the sovereign fashion of the Roman elite. In these canons we are dealing with a group process similar to the curial procedures of the later empire.

In the second place, the canons contain sufficient evidence to suggest that the crucial curial custom, according to which each member

5. Hess, pp. 30ff., 138; Roland Ganghoffer, *L'évolution des institutions municipales en occident et en orient au Bas-Empire* (Paris, 1962), with an excellent bibliography, pp. 1–22.

6. One perhaps should not use the term senatus consultum as an exact parallel to the canonic decisions, as Hamilton Hess does, because the concept actually belongs to the earlier empire (*CIL* 6.3823, 10.1401; cf. Francis de Zulueta, *The Institutes of Gaius* [Oxford, 1933], pp. 11, 15). Nevertheless, canons and senatus consulta result from similar decision-making processes (Pliny 2.19–23).

7. I read with Hefele (vol. 1, p. 221) *inter nos,* as suggested by H. Nolte, "Zur neuesten Bearbeitung der Synode von Elvira," *Theol. Quartalschrift* 41 (1865):309.

of the assembly had a right to bring up cases, was observed also by the council of Elvira.[8] The topical sequence of the canons betrays no overall planning. To be sure, several times, two subsequent canons deal with the same issue (19 and 20, 34 and 35, 49 and 50); once in a while, a series of canons treats the same subject (7ff., 63ff.); and the first four canons, on apostasy and the flaminate, certainly represent one topic. Such definite topical links, however, are only occasional. The canons show no sign that they were reordered after the council sessions. One can conclude safely that a coherent structuring of the debated material was not accomplished during the council and that the synod followed no agenda. It acted in the manner of a pagan curial procedure: each bishop or presbyter had his right to bring up cases for the synod's consideration.[9] It is no wonder that the canons open with the issue of apostasy and close with the unimportant one of women writing letters: can. 1 was brought up by one of the key men in Spanish Christianity to whom the floor was given first, while can. 81 was simply the last case brought to the floor by the last, if not the least, of the bishops.

Our understanding that neither the repetition nor the sequence of the issues was controlled represents a valuable opportunity to enter into the dynamic of the conciliar event, because it allows us to observe the leadership of the ancient church in a spontaneous action.[10] In the case of such spontaneity men are not merely talking in, or responding to, accepted and learned homiletical, moral, or theologi-

8. P. Batiffol, "Le règlement des premiers conciles africains," *Bulletin d'ancienne littérature et d'archéologie chrétienne* 3 (1913):3ff.; Robert M. Grant, *From Augustus to Constantine* (New York, 1970), p. 196.

9. A. Steinwenter, "Der antike kirchliche Rechtsgang und seine Quellen," *Zeitschrift der Savigny-Stiftung* 54, kan. Abtlg. 23 (1934):1ff. It cannot be determined to what degree bishops alone rather than bishops in cooperation with accompanying presbyters made the decisions (see Dale, p. 54). Both were present, and the presbyters "resided" *(residentibus)* with the bishops, as the Latin text claims; the deacons were described merely as *adstantibus* (J. D. Mansi, *Sacrorum Conciliorum Nova et Amplissima Collectio*, vol. 2 [Florence, 1759–98; Paris and Leipzig, 1901–27], col. 5); but since the canons protect and attack the bishops more than the presbyters, the former must have had more to say than the latter.

10. J. Gaudemet (*La formation du droit séculier et du droit de l'Eglise aux IVe et Ve siècles* [Paris, 1957]), although he deals with Elvira in several instances, begins his history of patristic conciliar law primarily with Arles (pp. 136ff.).

cal patterns, but are revealing their concerns and preferences without necessarily being aware of them. The comparisons will demonstrate the importance of such spontaneous elements, typical of the Romans' reluctance to systematize.[11] When I find, for instance, that over forty-five percent of these canons deal with the matter of sexuality, I have another such opportunity, for the bishops did not come to Elvira planning to spend almost half of their deliberations on sex. Whoever opened the debates began with the issues of apostasy and flaminate. The shift to sex was spontaneous, providing valuable evidence of the fears and longings of this early Christian elite.

In the third place, the canons exhibit certain patterns which appear again and again, patterns expressive of definite emotions, positions, and even group constellations within the synod. These it will be my task to isolate and identify. The canonic decisions seem at times antique examples for what is called today situational ethics.[12] Some canons denounce sinners without mercy, while others, for transgressions just as grave, make cautious qualifications. The discrepancies do not result from rational connection between crime and punishment. Rather the decisions vary according to the fluctuating emotional attitudes of the men making them. By separating language units into certain consistent patterns of expression, we can observe that what appears to be a conglomerate of arbitrary decisions were actually the juxtaposed verbalizations of emotions and positions in conflict, verbalizations resulting from the dramatic interrelations among the leaders who met at Elvira and, above all, between these leaders and their churches.

To be sure, the synod did not create its language or its procedure *ex nihilo*. The patterns and segments in these canons are the heritage of hundreds of years of tradition; they are Roman, Roman-Christian, Spanish-Roman-Christian.[13] When the council began by stating

11. Fritz Schulz, *Principles of Roman Law* (Oxford, 1936), pp. 53ff.

12. On the arbitrariness of the canons, observed even earlier by De Wette and Bauer, see Dale, pp. 96 and 104ff., and Hefele, p. 262.

13. The problem of the relation between provincial and traditional Roman law has not been solved satisfactorily (Gaudemet, p. 121).

placuit inter nos, it acted as a Roman-Christian assembly and employed age-old legal language.[14] Synods had met before.[15] What is unique in the canons of Elvira is their specific combinations of patterns and the applications of patterns to specific people and issues. The phrase, "nec in finem dandam esse communionem," for instance, was certainly not coined by this council; the council reserved it, however, for cases involving the three traditional capital sins of apostasy, adultery, and murder, with a definite emphasis on the first two. Similarly, the offering of grace in fine, that is, on the deathbed, had also been practiced before this council pronounced it.[16] Again, however, the synod applied such grace only in certain cases, never, for instance, to a cleric. When I can explain why the council operated with nec in finem at one instance and with in finem at another, I have found an access to the dynamic of the assembly.

Vital to an interpretation of these language patterns is the attribution to them of human experiences analogous to our own. When I interpret certain phenomena in the texts as experiences of the synod reflected in the texts, I do so by analogizing from my observations of the relationship between contemporary events and the documents recording them. The historian always works with such analogy, whether conscious of it or not. To give an example: when a church board or a political committee comes to certain decisions, and when we compare these decisions with what we remember or read about the meeting producing them, we realize the minutes are a distillation rather than a complete report of the meeting. Although the latter seem to represent univocal decisions, participants at such meetings know they actually are the result of negotiation, of victories by the

14. The basic framework of the Christian canons is Roman, but I also see elements that go back to the apodictic form of Jewish legislation present in ancient Christianity (see David Daube, *Forms of Roman Legislation* [Oxford, 1956], pp. 62ff.; and Gaudemet, p. 90).

15. Cyprian *Ep.* 67.5; *CSEL* 3.435ff.

16. On the use of tradition in Roman legal processes, see Max Kaser, *Das römische Zivilprozessrecht* (Munich, 1966), pp. 235ff. However, the Constantinian age began a period in imperial legal history marked by an astonishingly small number of lawyers who understood the Roman legal tradition (Max Kaser, *Römische Rechtsgeschichte* [Göttingen, 1965], p. 286).

majority, repressions of minority viewpoints as well as compromises. The language of texts like that of Elvira contains at times what the majority wanted to enforce and not what the assembly achieved, while in other cases the "decisions" are more expressions of anger, wishful thinking, political power-play, or personality clashes than indications of what the assembly actually wished to carry out. Many decisions which seem strange can be understood from the dynamic of the meetings that produced them. I have voted for resolutions which later I read with astonishment when they appeared in the minutes; they became comprehensible only when I recalled what went on during the meeting, who spoke for and who spoke against a certain matter, and what my own personal involvement was at that moment. From my knowledge of the relationship between the modern text and the group producing it, I can draw certain conclusions about the relationship between the canons of Elvira and the synod of Elvira, although this synod is an unknown. Thus, a contemporary text stands in the same relation to a contemporary group as the canons of Elvira stand to the synod of Elvira.

Such historical analogy assumes a universality of human interactive behavior over the span of two millenia: uncertainty and spontaneity were operating among the bishops who came to a basilica in southern Spain not so differently from the way they operate when we fly to Geneva or New York for a meeting of the World Council of Churches. In antiquity, as now, hope and fear, coercion and compromise, traditional reluctance and historical dynamism found their locus, their expression, and their reflection in the word, the phrase, the sentence, the model. To be sure, the interactions responsible for words and sentences may not follow precisely the same rules. It may even be that psychic mutations are gradually occurring in human beings. For this reason I define the historical experiment as one employing not simple analogy, but proportional analogy, to adopt a Thomistic phrase. In such proportionality I presuppose similar reactions in antique and modern man, although I concede that mutations in the human structures do occur and that therefore social and psychological reactions may not be exactly the same at different stages of historical processes.

The correlation and tension between analogy, which is possible because of historical continuity, and proportionality, which reckons with the mutation in historical evolution, underlies the problem of history. I feel part of the past, yet I also experience the break with the past. I walk through the blocks of Leptis Magna and Djemila: in cities like these the bishops of Elvira's churches ruled their flocks. Imperial cities, *decumanus* and *cardo,* mosaics, nymphaea, altars, theaters. Roman inscriptions suggestive of the imperial-religious ideology: *flamen perpetuus.* My imagination begins to work: all the problems with which I struggle in the canons of Elvira are visibly laid out here. In the forum of Timgad is evidence of one of the many third-century inscriptions in which the name of a soldier-emperor was chiseled out. What was taking place in this century that a man's name could be damned to be forgotten? The deed repels me: this is not my world anymore. But the deed also evokes experiences in my own life. Index of prohibited writings. Heinrich Heine banned from bookstores. Mendelssohn forbidden in concert programs. Trotski's name crossed off, forgotten. By a complicated process of analogy, I think myself into the remote and yet familiar age of soldier-emperors, partly by intuiting in it a set of shifting elements similar to those going on in my own time. I try to recapture the life in Sabratha's third-century cultures by letting my imagination and experience play into the tangible evidences, the brick, the arenas, the inscriptions, and the art and artifacts of the late antique world.

It is easy to be afraid of committing oneself and to limit one's interpretations of historical matter to what can be demonstrated unassailably. The attempts to capture life situations in their social and psychological dynamic are often so elusive and necessarily tentative. But the attempts to enter the world of Elvira need not be much more tentative than trying to come to terms with contemporary life. The difference between being able to understand a canon of Elvira and a contemporary statesman's declaration is one only of degree. Can. 36

of Elvira declares: "There shall be no pictures in churches lest what is worshipped and adored be depicted on walls." Richard Nixon declares: "We are neither pro-Arab nor pro-Israel. We are pro-peace. We are for security for all the nations in the area."[17] Although we have much more material on the latter, the problem remains basically the same: the words are true and false at the same time. To understand the paradox of words is to break out of one's sphere and to experience the human struggle, both critically and imaginatively. Historiography is ambiguous because life is ambiguous, because the human personality and hence man's language and his relation to his world are immensely complicated. The canons of Elvira are a cryptic document and the contextual evidence is relatively scarce. But the evidence suffices to permit a reconstruction of that striking council in terms of the human encounter, a scene in the drama of the closing centuries of the ancient world.

17. "Quotation of the Day," *New York Times*, 31 January 1970, p. 29.

Two

THE AMBIGUITY OF DECISION

The point from which to start an analysis of the event of 309 is with the conciliar language itself, in which one encounters a political drive for power as well as the ambiguities arising out of conflicting values, and then the compromises which are typical in every decision-making process. These canons, which are distillations out of human interactions among the clerical elite present in the synodal sessions, have an identifiable rhythm, and their decisions have identifiable patterns. The language of these canons displays a rhythm of curt simplicity,[1] which can be identfed by means of separating the canons into simple linguistic units, s^1 through s^5, consisting of a word, a series of words, or an entire clause:

> s^1: the person: *a flamen*
> s^2: the cause: *who after baptism has sacrificed*
> s^3: the justification: *since he committed such a crime*
> s^4: the authority: *we have decided*
> s^5: the decision: *shall not receive communion*

Such is, in abbreviated form, the fivefold rhythm of can. 2, for example. The segments represent the basic rhetorical thrust of a canon, although not every segment is present in every canon.[2] The rhythm

---

1. This rhythmic rhetoric is found in old Roman texts (see, for example, *Lex Aquil.* IX. 2, *fragm.* 11.1). Roman legal language contained both simplicity (Schulz, *Principles of Roman Law*, pp. 66ff.) and verbosity (J. Marouzeau, "Sur deux aspects de la language du droit," *Droits de l'antiquité et sociologie juridique: Mélanges Lévy-Bruhl* [Paris, 1959] pp. 435ff.).

2. Segments s^2, s^3, and s^4 are those most frequently omitted. There are also frequent inversions: s^2, s^1, s^4, s^5, s^3.

conveys the force by which the assembly asserted its power over the church.

One can analyze the decisions proper by subdividing the s^5 segments into six basic patterns according to their degree of severity or leniency, the variousness of their purpose and intensity. The language of the segments s^1 through s^4 indicates a council certain of its ground in confronting the problems before it. The decision patterns, however, are full of ambiguity, mixing fear with hope, and vague prohibitions with determined penalties. The range of decision patterns—d^1 through d^6—shows the wide gap that exists between such injunctions as "They shall abstain" and "They shall not receive communion, not even at the end." The segments express how the council confronted the problems and arrived at a decision. On the face of it, the canons exhibit certainty, even dogmatism. A close analysis of the decision patterns, however, reveals an astonishing complexity and indeterminateness in the attitudes of the clerics who passed judgment. The rhythmic motion from s^1 to s^5 demonstrates vividly the synod's drive toward power, but the range of purpose and meaning in the six decision patterns points to an inner turmoil that was present not only in that assembly which meant to assert its authority, but in the Spanish churches in general.

THE LANGUAGE SEGMENTS

It was not new for the language of law to have a rhetorical rhythm of tart, cryptic brevity: the Twelve Tablets of ancient Rome had a short, concise form, and so did the Decalogue. The canons of Elvira, however, in their unsophisticated, popular Latin phraseology, permit us to read evidence of group processes.[3] The rhythm suits an elite trying to impose its will on the church at a moment of crucial change. By rhythm I do not mean metrics, but the rhetorical accents and emphases comprising the language units by which the assembly com-

3. The canons have the primitive legal character of Constantinian vulgar law with its lack of consistency and immoderate threats of punishments (Wolfgang Kunkel, *An Introduction to Roman Legal and Constitutional History* [Oxford, 1966], p. 144).

municated its determination to govern the church. This kind of canonical speech is somewhat like the asyndetic diction of ancient hymnody in that it combines blocks of words into rhythmical units. Yet, unlike ancient hymnody, it is not poetic but cast in the prose of rhetoric, expressing thereby the confrontation between lawgiver and subordinate, assembly and people. Although legal language tends to become ornate and intricate, the language of these canons remained primitive and simple. It expressed the charge of clerical leaders, sitting, if one can trust the text, in the exedra of a Spanish basilica, to the *ecclesia*, the laymen sitting in the nave and representing the audience of Spanish Christianity. In the rhythmic segments one can hear the bishops and presbyters calling out and giving orders to their troubled churches.

The simplicity of the syntax may be related, in part, to the limited education of many of the bishops present. It is also related, however, to the existential character of these canons. They are phrased in the language of immediate experience, and the syntax of such experiential language is simple and concrete.[4] The syntax of legal sentences becomes complex when it is self-consciously pondered over, intellectualized, and hence abstracted. The canons of Elvira allow a somewhat successful reconstruction of the event because they are free of such retrospective theological, legal, or ethical sophistication. In them we see the free play of personal and social forces. The bishops and the presbyters at Elvira did not cogitate in the manner of canon lawyers; they acted.

The Person—s[1]

The canons frequently begin by naming a person as the culprit before the assembly: matrons (57), priests (55), adolescents (31), freedmen (80). In the very positioning of the name, there is implied an emo-

---

4. The cryptic (6, 43), sometimes crude (15) or even unclear (26), quality of the canons contrasts with the verbosity of the imperial decisions of the age (e.g., *Cod. Just.* IX.18.4).

tional accent, a charge: Here we name you. It is as if the wording of the decision were specifically designed to identify the object of the canon, the "against whom" it is directed, a human being or group, as a foe.[5] In accordance with Roman legal tradition, the "against whom" was not an abstraction but a specific title or category of persons: in the singular, it may be a catechumen (68) or magistrate (56); in the plural, false witnesses (74) or deacons (77). It is possible that when a singular was used the bishop proposing the sententia had a particular individual in mind, while the plural was directed against a specific group of people.

This naming of a person at the outset of a canon signals the involvement of the church leaders with individuals and groups at the moment they formulated their decisions. The opening phrase—"If some widow" (72), "If some woman" (5)—is the first step toward an action, toward a relationship either of control or of acceptance.[6] The solemn assembly hurled its anger against its real or imagined enemies: "a baptized woman who" (9), "someone among the faithful" (46).[7] To be sure, the s^1 segments employ at times the less specific pronoun: "all those who" (24), "someone" (60), "those who" (52).[8] In the latter cases, the total emphasis falls on the next segment, yet even here the canons point toward a person and not toward an issue. They do not say: No sacrificing! (1), It is prohibited to enter the forum while sacrifices are taking place (59), Abortion is punishable by full exclusion from the communion of the church (68). Instead the charges are directed against people: "anyone . . . from the Catholic church" (22).

One hears in the opening segments of the canons the range of personal and social conflicts taking place during that assembly. The

5. The canons show the Roman concern for specific cases rather than abstractions (Schulz, pp. 40ff.).

6. For the Roman preoccupation with *actiones* in jurisprudence, see the discussion of the old Roman *legis actiones* in Max Kaser, *Das altrömische Jus* (Göttingen, 1949), pp. 72–73; Schulz, p. 42.

7. For Roman parallels, cf. *Lex. Áquil.* IX. 2, *fragm.* 56 (*mulier si*), *fragm.* 23 (*si servus*), *fragm.* 5.3 (*si magister*), *fragm.* 7.8 (*si medicus*).

8. *Lex. Aquil.* IX. 2, *fragm.* 11.1 (*si alius*), *fragm.* 7.2ff. (*si quis*).

subjects of the s^1 units are, for instance, the rich (29), the ill (37), public officials (56), the average girl (14) and the average boy (31). They include converts (39), either from paganism (2ff.) or from heretical communities (22), people either on the periphery of the church (21), or those within the hierarchy [subdeacons (29), presbyters (32), bishops (27)] and also the average faithful (5). They are all people within the church, or at least people in the process of entering the church. The conflict in the drama of Elvira was not between the church and the world, but between the assembly and a great number of individuals within the Christian church.

The Cause—s^2

In the second segment, s^2, following the naming of the person, the issue is named. The assembly put the bell on the neck of the cat: s^1, flamines, s^2, who have sacrificed (2); s^1, virgins, s^2, who do not keep their virginity (14). The second segments represent a second accent, a second tone. After naming the culprit, the synod declared what the culprit did; where in the first segment it experienced the conflict with persons, it experienced in the second the conflict in regard to deeds: sacrifice, usury, divorce, dice-playing. The syntax shows the order of the synod's action, from exposing the person (flamines) to condemning the deed (who sacrificed). Separating the opening of the canons into these two parts illustrates how complicated social and psychological processes were taking place in the course of that council. The church was plagued by a web of personality clashes and by conflicting social attitudes. Yet the synod's conflict with persons can not always be correlated with its treatment of issues, for women are treated differently in some canons than in others, and so are flamines and priests. The decisions respond at times to personal issues, at times to material ones, and at times to both. Furthermore, the step from s^1 to s^2 was not always an action from accusing a person to naming the transgression [bishops who were caught in sexual transgressions (18)], but could move from naming a person to spelling out an exculpating circumstance [a catechumen who should fall gravely ill (11)]. What is vital to observe is the rhythmic similarity in the movement from s^1 to s^2, whether it leads from the person to the sin, or from the person to the excuse. Whether the clerics are meting out punishment or dispensing mercy, they are exercising control. It is this control which is disclosed by the language rhythm.

Syntactically, the relationship between s^1 and s^2 has the basic types presented in abbreviated form in table 1. The mentioning of the per-

TABLE 1

SYNTACTICAL RELATIONSHIP BETWEEN s^1 AND s^2

s^1	s^2	Canon
flamines	qui sacrificaverunt	2
flamines	si fuerint	4
omnes qui	fuerint baptizati	24
si quis	fecerit	22
		42
magistratus	uno anno quo agit	56
stupratoribus puerum	. . .	71

son, in s^1, can be followed, in s^2, by a *qui* clause, a *si* clause or, as is frequently the case, a combination of qui and si (42). The si clause often modifies or weakens the qui clause (13). There are only a few cases where the entire condemnation is implied in s^1, and s^2 is not needed (27, 71).

There are only a few cases where s^1 is omitted and where the emphasis lies on an abstract issue and not on a person: in can. 23, dealing with the days of fasting *(jejunii superpositiones);* in 26, relating this same practice of fasting to the sabbath; in 34, prohibiting the placing of candles in cemeteries; in 36, speaking against pictures in churches. The second part of can. 48 belongs to the same exception: feet are not to be washed. On the other hand, the second part of 34 contains an s^2 segment. In any case, exceedingly few of these 81 canons deal with a problem abstractly, outside a personal confrontation. The overwhelming majority of canons proceed from person to deed.

In this language process, s^1 and s^2, lay the first stage of the synodal process.[9] When the synod began to deal with a case, it began to act. It attacked, it manipulated, it qualified. Whether in hostility or mercy, the synod related, or tried to relate, to certain groups or individuals in its midst and in its churches. It is in this attempt to relate that one can read the synod's effort to establish itself as an elite force in a time of crisis and change.

The Justification—s^3

The naming of the culprit, s^1, and of the ground for his condemnation, s^2, is followed by the sanction against the offender. In about one-third of the canons, however, a highly emotional phrase intervenes which does not belong to the decision proper, but which justifies the sanction by some exclamation of horror: "and commits this major crime" (1). These segments, which either precede or follow the decisions, will be represented by s^3. Of the twenty-eight canons in which they are found, in sixteen they are introduced by *eo quod*, in six by *ne*, and in three by *propter*. I list the segments here:

```
 1: quia est summi sceleris
 2: eo quod geminaverint ... vel triplicaverint
 6: eo quod sine idololatria perficere scelus non potuit
12: eo quod alium vendiderit corpus vel potius suum
13: eo quod lapsae potius videantur
13: non intelligentes quid admiserint
14: eo quod solas nuptias violaverint
14: eo quod moechatae sunt
15: propter copiam puellarum
15: ne aetas in flore tumens in adulterium animae resolvatur
16: eo quod nulla possit societas fideli cum infideli
```

9. In can. 15, *propter* makes no sense. The word could be the error of a scribe; however, it could also be the result of the debates, a slip of the tongue: "because of the abundance of girls," instead of "despite the abundance of girls." The five-year penalty in can. 11 seems to come from nowhere, possibly because part of can. 11 is lost, or because of the unsystematic way the canons were written down. In this case, 11 continued what was debated in 10b.

18: propter scandalum et propter profanum crimen
21: ut correptus esse videatur
22: eo quod cognoverit peccatum suum
22: quod non suo vitio peccaverint
23: propter quorundam infirmitatem
24: eo quod eorum minime sit cognita vita
25: eo quod omnes sub hac nominis gloriae passim concutiant simplices
30: eo quod postmodum per subreptionem ad altiorem gradum promoveantur
34: inquietandi enim sanctorum spiritus non sunt
35: eo quod saepe sub obtenu orationis latenter scelera committunt
36: ne quod colitur et adoratur in parietibus depingatur
43: juxta auctoritatem scriptorum
43: ne si quis non fecerit
45: eo quod veterem hominem novam heresim induxisse notetur
48: ne sacerdos quod gratia accepit pretio distrahere videatur
49: ne nostram irritam et infirmam faciant benedictionem
59: quod si fecerit, pari crimine teneatur
60: quatenus in Evangelio scriptum non est neque invenietur sub apostolis umquam factum
63: eo quod geminaverit scelus
65: ne ab his qui exemplum bonae conversationis esse debent, ab eis videantur secelerum magisterium procedere
66: eo quod sit incestus

These s^3 segments are parenthetical appeals, intended to reinforce the impact of the decision. They span a wide range of emotional attitudes, from the rational plea for leniency in treating the children of heretics: "since they have not sinned on their own" (22), to the irrational outcries (12, 59, 63) which contribute nothing to the content of the canon but simply express disgust and horror: "because of the scandal and the heinousness of the crime" (18). With such polemic, the synod seems to have felt, a sentence would persuade the people of the rightness of the judgment or frighten them from committing similar crimes. The clerics used at times quite practical arguments: think about the abundance of Christian girls and you will understand why we need to prohibit marriage between Christians and pagans (15). Also they did not shy away from bigotry—Don't let the blessings of the Jews invalidate your own Christian blessings (49)— or from popular magical superstition—You should not disturb the spirits of the dead (34).

The majority of these exclamatory justifications and warnings as persuasive levers represent common sense or emotional reactions to cases in question. Only 4 of these 31 segments have theological or scriptural sources. One mentions *scriptura* (43), another, *evangelium* (60), and two quote scriptural passages (16, 45). This means that only five percent of the canons of Elvira cite scriptural justifications. Apparently the bishops did not need theology or scripture to undergird their authority. One could understand this lack of scriptural support easily if the council had made no such references at all; one could also understand if scripture were called on only in support of pivotal issues, or some especially hard decision. Neither, however, is the case. There is no correlation between the presence of a scriptural segment in a canon and the importance of that canon's topic.

Twenty-eight of these eighty-one canons contain an s^3 phrase. Why do not the rest? One would be led to suspect that crucial subject matters or touchy decisions necessitated the additional support. Again, there is no evidence for such an assumption. Some of the harshest anathemas make use of an s^3 unit; others, just as severe, and just as basic to the tenor of the assembly, do not. One can conclude, therefore, that in the spontaneous procedure of this council such a segment was interjected when someone, perhaps the man responsible for bringing up the *sententia*, was moved to insist that the phrase be put in. The distribution of these justifying clauses indicates that some of the bishops or presbyters in the council were less prone than others to use such emotional appeals, for 7–11, 26–29, 37–42, and 67–81 have no s^3 segments. Furthermore, the fact that these segments become rarer toward the end of the synod is a comment on the overall condition of the council. The clergy of Elvira, like most of us who have to attend meetings lasting for hours or days, became fatigued toward the end of the synod. The last fifteen canons, although they express many strict measures, contain no s^3 units.

The analysis of these justifying clauses brings up the problems of identity and security, with which I shall deal later. These s^3 segments are important not so much because of their content, but because of what they say about the men who proposed them. It is quite probable that these justifying clauses were interjected to counter the uncertainty of the individual proponent. To give an example, the person interjecting the phrase "scandal and crime" in can. 18 needed that additional exclamation of disgust in order to silence some latent protest and to convince not only the brethren but perhaps himself of the justice in the levy. These erratic s^3 units, often rather innocuous or obvious, do not really give any rational support to the decision; their presence and form illuminate the contrast between the external confidence displayed in the rhythmic force of the canonic segments, and the tentativeness displayed in the decision patterns. They are valuable evidence for the council's mixture of confidence and uncertainty.

The Authority—s^4

For the fourth segment we can single out the word "placuit."[10] In the rhythmic fluctuation of the canon, placuit expressed the assurance of the righteous amid the turmoil, multiplicity, and dissent that is represented in s^1 and s^2 and the tensions which are hidden under various patterns of s^5. In pronouncing the placuit, the council acted as the leadership group and set itself apart from all the people it meant to discipline, laity and pagans, rebellious bishops and faithless converts. As he cried this placuit into the basilica, or voted for the decision undergirded by the placuit, the individual cleric identified with the judicial majority: *placuit cunctis* (53). When the synod began with the words: placuit inter nos, it said in fact: we decide what follows; we, a Roman assembly; we, the power elite of the church;

10. A. Berger, *Encyclopedic Dictionary of Roman Law,* (Philadelphia, 1953), p. 632.

and you had better not argue with such superior authority.[11] It is quite another matter to ask if the sanctions that followed sustained such a mood of assurance. As we shall see, they did not. But at the s^4 moment of the language rhythm, in the seconds when placuit was pronounced, the synod felt the titillation of power, daring to steer the religious destiny of its provinces.

The position of placuit in the structure of the individual canons supports my understanding of the emotional weight of the word. Only four times does the word appear in the beginning of a canon (33, 36, 53, 58); only four times does it appear in second place (40, 41, 48, 49).[12] In all other cases, placuit is placed at a later accent in the canon's rhythm, representing a platform for the decision after the first two segments are established. Can. 1 demonstrates the function of placuit very clearly. It starts out with the phrase placuit inter nos, thereby establishing the base for the decision-making process of the synod; then, just before the sanction it repeats the word: "placuit nec in finem eum communionem accipere." The first placuit established the group's intention to make pronouncements, *urbi et orbi*, to all the people present in the church and to those in the Spanish churches back home; the second placuit established that intention for the specific, concrete case in can. 1. While the opening phrase served as the plinth on which the synod meant to put the entire legal structure, the second placuit already belonged to a specific decision, and in the sequence of that decision the person and issue came first.

This s^4 segment appears in fifty-seven canons. Does that mean that the twenty-four canons which do not have this segment are somewhat less important? There is not the slightest evidence to support such a differentiation. Frequently the infinitive construction of a canon assumes a placuit without naming it. Some highly important

11. The authority and meaning of this placuit belong to the specific authority displayed at Elvira. The authority of later councils, such as Nicaea, Tyre, Ephesus, Constantinople, shows a constant shift toward greater autocracy in the church.

12. That canons having placuit in first or second place are in rather close proximity to each other argues that they may have been phrased by the same cleric, or clerics, and that the proposer felt somewhat different from the others.

canons leave it out and some unimportant ones do likewise. While many of these canons consist of two or even three sentences, only three canons (3, 13, 20) repeat an s^4 segment. All other canons with two decisions introduce placuit either for the first decision (73) or for the second (74). Obviously it sufficed to phrase this word once since it served as the group's point of stability, an affirmation of strength before the critical moment of decision.

The Decision—s^5

The critical moment did come: pronouncements were made, out of the complicated maze of canonic decisions vibrating from the storms of the ancient church. To decipher that maze is no easy task. What is a decision? Certainly it is not an isolated sentence. From what has been established thus far, one can see that the canons are polemical, rhythmic reflections of conflicts and emotions, expressions of an event in a Spanish basilica in which a group of Christian leaders yelled its anger and asserted its will.[13] The decision is the climax in that rhythmic experience, the final breath of an address in which bishops and presbyters directly confronted their flocks. Compare, for instance, two extreme levies, on the one hand the canon which pronounces an uncompromising exclusion from the church, and on the other that which demands the unconditioned acceptance of a questionable person back into the church. The canon which contains the radical anathema: "If a man/marries his step-daughter/he shall not be given communion even at the end" (66) has the same rhythm as the canon offering acceptance: "A prostitute/if afterwards she has come to belief/shall be received without delay" (44).

If the same rhythm leads to anathema as well as to mercy and, of course, to the many nuances between the two, then the fact that the clerics spoke either negatively or positively about issues is at first less

---

13. The internal conflicts in the Spanish churches can be traced to at least half a century before Elvira, as revealed by the deposition of the bishops of Legia Asturica and Emerita (Cyprian, *Ep.* 3).

important than the fact that they spoke in the same rhythm. The clerics acted. A decision is an action. It is also a reaction, to Christians present and not present; it is an expression of hope and anxiety, but it implies also a social thrust: the clerics, in warning the people to whom they conveyed their decisions, led them and controlled. A "decision" is therefore an exceedingly complex mixture of formalized, traditional resolutions and language patterns, of explicit and implicit reactions to threatening problems, by means of which the clerics attempted to secure or enhance their leadership in vital spheres of daily life. In order to decode the enigma of these decisions, separating them into distinct categories will reveal that the seemingly arbitrarily connected legal phrases actually form certain logical patterns of reactions to urgent problems and of attempts to govern the Christian church.

Six different patterns can be identified in these canonic decisions. One expresses a peremptory injunction: This shall be done. There is no qualification, no threat, no penance. The synod prescribes the behavior it requires. I call this first pattern decision one (d^1). In addition, four negative patterns should be distinguished carefully from each other. Some decisions say merely: They must do this. Some, however, add a threat: They must do this, otherwise we shall throw them out. There are punitive decisions: If they do this, we shall punish them. And there are decisions that levy a most extreme penalty: If they do this, they shall not be taken back even on their deathbed. These four negative patterns, which will be designated by d^2 through d^5, exhibit subtle and significant nuances and reveal a web of intention and reaction: determined leadership, angry enforcement of moral postulates, utopian hopes, threats. There also exists, however, a reluctantly positive pattern, a mitigation of the negative pronouncements: We may take them back at the end. This pattern will be designated d^6. These patterns, intermingled throughout the corpus of Elvira, provide an insight into the working of the synod, and illuminate the ambiguity of the text. They enable the reader to study the anxiety and tentativeness on the part of the men who made these decisions as well as to measure the intensity of the drive with which the early Christian elite took on its task of leadership. The division into such patterns makes it clear that in the penitential language of the church the command to anathematize, discipline, or punish does not mean that anathema, discipline, or penalty were carried out *eo ipso*. Out of context, when separated, the patterns state prohibitions. Since some patterns have considerably stronger sanctions than others, however, they clearly can not be taken at face value. As the analysis will show, every one of these decision patterns is in itself ambiguous. A pattern seldom means one thing, which is why it does not allow a simplistic reading. When the ancient church said No, it did not mean necessarily a categorical injunction. The No had a variety of resonances indicative of a wide range of hopes and fears. A comparative analysis of decision patterns makes it possible to distinguish one No from another.

THE DECISION PATTERNS

d^1: This shall be done.
d^2: They must not do this.
d^3: If they do this, we shall throw them out.
d^4: If they do this, they must do penance.
d^5: If they do this, there shall be no mercy even at the end.
d^6: Under the pressure of illness, there shall be mercy on their deathbed.

Although some canons represent border cases, the majority of decisions clearly can be attributed to one of the six patterns (see table 2). Since the eighty-one canons actually contain 134 decisions, many of the canons are subdivided into separate decisions, for instance, 37a, 37b, 37c.

This Shall Be Done—d^1

The first pattern represents the imperative This shall be done. Expressing the social code by apodictic-positive command has always been part of the legal enterprise: Honor your father and your mother.

The synod employed it when it regulated the observance of liturgical customs [Pentecost (43) and fasting (23, 26)] and when it made demands on the daily lives of catechumens (77), laymen (25, 58), and bishops (19b, 27a). Especially significant is the use of this pattern in two canons in which controversial people are invited to enter the church without penitential requirements: a prostitute who marries a

TABLE 2

OCCURENCES OF THE DECISION PATTERNS

d^1	d^2		d^3	d^4		d^5	d^6
10a	9a	48b	20a	4	57b	1	3a
19b	15	49a	20c	5a	59b	2	5c
20b	16a	51a	30b	5b	61a	3b	9c
22c	16b	53b	33b	9b	62a	6	10b
23	19a	57a	34b	14a	64b	7	11
25	24	59a	37c	14b	69a	8	13b
26	27a	60	41c	16c	70b	12	32b
41b	27b	67a	49b	21	72a	13a	37a
43	28	80	51b	22a	72c	17	38
44	29a	81a	52	22b	73b	18	39
45	29b	81b	62b	31	73c	47b	42b
53a	30a		67b	32a	74b	63	47a
58	33a		74a	40b	74c	64a	54b
77	34a		78a	42a	76a	65	61b
	35		79a	46	76b	66	68
	36			50	78b	70a	69b
	37b			54a	79b	71	72d
	40a			54c		72b	
	41a			55		73	
	48a			56		75	

NOTE: Of the 134 decisions, there are fourteen occurrences of d^1, thirty-one of d^2, fifteen of d^3, thirty-seven of d^4, twenty of d^5, and seventeen of d^6.

husband and comes to faith shall instantly be accepted into the church (44); a catechumen who has not gone to church but who has led a good life shall not be denied baptism (45). In these imperative decisions the synod not only expressed apodictic commands to regulate the life of the churches, but also was invitational, offering acceptance not always allowed to individuals.

To be sure, such affirmative function in canonic language is rare. The majority of other canons contain either negative decisions (d^2 through d^5) or qualifications of negative decisions (d^6). The difference between operating with apodictic-positive and apodictic-negative patterns is the difference between leading the community by positive suggestions and leading it by negative reactions, imposing fear and threat. It is amazing that the positive-apodictic approach exists at all, and even more amazing that there are signs of an invitational-accepting positive pattern which only in recent times has begun to play a major role in leadership and educational methods. The positive pattern does not have a major function in the synod of Elvira. Only fourteen of 134 decisions make use of it, and only eight of the eighty-one canons consist solely of this type of decision. The purely invitational type, as exemplified by 44 and 45, is even rarer. Typical of ancient canonic assemblies, this synod controlled its churches primarily by negation and prohibition, disciplining and punishing its flock, and only rarely offering affirmative solutions to communal difficulties. The power of the clerical elite rested in the No.

A large part of these d^1 decisions appears in two groups: 22c, 23, 25, 26, and 41b, 43, 44, 45. This arresting fact certainly can not be a matter of coincidence. Perhaps when these d^1 phrases were pronounced, the synod was in a different mood than it was at other periods of its procedure. Perhaps the bishops who brought up the subjects of these canons were more affirming leaders who were speaking less than others out of negative reactions, or perhaps the men who reacted to these subjects by offering mitigating sentences were more affirming than others. In any case, the emotional mood displayed in these two groups of canons was more positive than elsewhere.[14] This

14. The insights in this paragraph are based, of course, on the assumption, there being no evidence to the contrary, that the sequence of the canons as preserved in the manuscripts is the original one and had not been tampered with to any great extent later on. The impressive comparisons which J. Gaudemet ("Elvire," 347) has made between the decisions of Elvira and the Gratian texts support strongly the assumption that the fourth century preserved the canons of Elvira rather faithfully.

observation has implications for an evaluation of certain canons. Why, for instance, did the prostitute of can. 44 get off so easily, quite unexpectedly in view of the puritanical and antisexual decisions before and afterwards? Was it simply by chance? Whatever the cause, when the synod phrased can. 44, it was in a more irenic stage than it had been before and was to be afterwards. One wonders why. One also could conjecture that had 27, the canon demanding that only a sister or a dedicated virgin daughter live with a cleric, appeared at another point in the proceedings, it might have been phrased in a more punitive way.

They Must Not Do This—d²

The canons of Elvira contain four different patterns by means of which a certain deed or behavior is rejected. Pattern d^2 represents a canon or part of a canon in which a straightforward prohibition is stated: "They must not do this." While many other canons threaten the transgressor either with a sentence of exclusion or of penance, the d^2 sentences stop at the prohibition, not reckoning with the chance that it may not be heeded. Why not? Is the difference between canons that merely say No and canons that carefully spell out what happens when Christians disregard the No a matter of chance? Is it that some of the men who formulated particular sentences happened to reckon with disobedience while others did not? It can be shown that the difference is not merely coincidental, and results from the bishops' ambivalence. In some canons the simple prohibition sufficed because the synod did not fear noncompliance. In others, however, the synod failed to spell out penalty, exclusion, or mercy because the clerics were uncertain about their own convictions.

The famous can. 36 illustrates this first of Elvira's four negative patterns: "There shall be no pictures in churches, lest what is worshipped and adored be depicted on walls." The text has been controversial in historical analysis, in respect to Christian art and ancient Christian iconoclasm, because it does not make clear what the problem of iconoclasm was in Spain at the time.[15] Were all images summarily banned or only those with liturgical connotations? Did the canon attack abuses or did it presuppose the total absence of art in churches? I believe that the ambiguity of the decision is revealing: it was in such a d^2 pattern that the synod operated when it did not want to commit itself.

There are three kinds of ambiguity in can. 36. In the first place, the canon has no addressee; it is one of the few canons which deal merely with the issue, without an s^1 segment. The canon, however, should have an s^1 segment, for those walls on which pictures were not to be painted were surely not decorated by angels. Bishops and presbyters, the same kinds of people who made decisions at Elvira, decided on such matters. When the synod meant to stop either a cleric or a layman from committing some objectionable deed, it certainly named him, or her, or them: "Bishops and presbyters who. . . ." Yet in the canon under discussion, the synod did not come to terms with persons. In the second place, the canon has no sanction. When the synod was afraid that its decision would not be heeded, it certainly was not reluctant to outline penalty or anathema, as the forty-nine cases of penance and irrevocable exclusion show. It does not spell out what would happen if images were put into churches. Moreover, in leaving out the s^1 unit, the synod did not even hold anyone responsible for such a misdeed. In the third place, the canon has a rather puzzling s^3 segment: "ne quod colitur et adoretur in parietibus depingatur." This segment could be interpreted as meaning that only what might be worshipped and adored was prohibited; but the main part of the canon does not prohibit images in such a restricted way. The synod's ambivalence is unmistakable.

These three evidences, compared to the other decision patterns, make it quite clear that in the decision in can. 36 the synod was un-

15. Hugo Koch, *Die altchristliche Bilderfrage nach den litterarischen Quellen* (Göttingen, 1917), pp. 31ff.; W. Elliger, *Die Stellung der alten Christen zu den Bildern* (Leipzig, 1930), pp. 34ff.

willing to commit itself. Why? There are two possibilities: either it did not regard the issues as very important, and did not expect much resistance, or it felt that the issue was too hot and it did not dare to make stringent sanctions against disobedience. One has to reckon, in all of the d^2 decisions, with both of these possibilities. They are not as unlike each other as one assumes at first sight. Whether the synod regarded the case under scrutiny as too unimportant to make an issue of or only halfheartedly supported its own ruling does not matter. What matters is that sanctions, anathema, and penance were left out of the d^2 decisions. They were left out to avert a confrontation.

Such evasion is especially clear in can. 36. The decision is ambiguous because the synod did not want to use the iconoclastic issue as a test case of its control of the churches. For some reasons that can no longer be recovered the issue came up in the council. It found a majority vote, perhaps a unanimous one. Who knows? The verdict, however, was vague: no one was threatened, no one was to be punished. The decision, like the preceding s^3 segment, was inconclusive, and this canon was the only one passed concerning the matter of iconoclasm.[16] The clerics who came to Elvira did not want to make a major issue out of iconoclasm. Perhaps they themselves loved images, their aesthetic character, their symbolic beauty. Perhaps there were pictures in their own churches which they felt were harmless. Yet they could imagine abuses, and so a stance had to be taken. The fourth-century church profited from their tentativeness: images became acceptable.[17]

This tentativeness can be understood when set against the background of early Christianity's relationship to art. Ever since the beginning of Christianity there had been polemic by Christian writers against the use of images, which was inherited in part from Judaism and in part from the philosophical criticism of popular religion.[18] The

16. Can. 52 on satirical writings is, at most, related only remotely to the issue of images.

17. J. Kollwitz, "Bild," *Reallexikon für Antike und Christentum,* 2, col. 329–30.

18. Heraclitus, *fragm.* 5; Zenon, *fragm.* 264; Herodotus 1.131; Seneca in Lact. *Inst.* VI.25.3; M. Höpfner, *Reallexikon für Antike und Christentum,* 2, col. 315.

critical statements of the early church against image worship were made by theologians, by the Christian leaders who rejected images as pagan, idolatrous, blasphemous, anthropomorphic, and crass.[19] The archeological evidence, however, shows that Christianity in the third century, if not earlier, often produced pictures. The catacombs are full of them, and the baptistry and sanctuary at Duro Europos exhibit them. Can. 36 of Elvira would not have been necessary if pictures had not existed at all.

The conflict about images is related to the different attitudes toward them among clergy and laity. While the Christian elite regarded the icons for a long time with hostility, the Christian grass-roots community employed them without qualm.[20] The conflict between traditional clerical anti-iconic positions and the popular demand for images was in evidence only a few years after Elvira when Constantine asked Eusebius of Caesarea for a picture of Christ, and Eusebius although one of the protagonists for Constantine's imperial Christian ideals, rejected the emperor's demand. For centuries, an anti-iconic and a pro-iconic stance continued side by side in the Christian church, one leading to the superb art of Ravenna and the other to the iconoclastic pogroms of the eighth century. The dilemma of can. 36 is the dilemma of a crucial moment involving that duality.

The ambiguity of can. 36, thus, directly reflects the mixed feelings of the clergy toward the matter. As members of the Christian elite, they had to speak against the images; as part of a church that acquiesced more and more in the popular demand for visual, concrete imagery, they were not so sure about the corrupting character of such art. The d^2 decision of can. 36 enables us to read that ambivalence between the elite's traditional theological, as well as social, rejection of images and its personal emotional acceptance of them.

The d^2 pattern, therefore, was applied to cases that were easily resolvable because the persons named were essentially powerless to

19. Theophilus *Ad Aut.* 2.2; Origen *Contra Celsum* 6.66; Tertullian *De Idol.* 1ff.
20. Kollwitz, 2, col. 321.

resist. It was also applied, however, to precisely opposite cases in which obedience would have been very hard to secure. Can. 29, for instance, prohibiting possessed Christians from participating in the liturgy of the church or from holding an office in the church, did not need to say more. The mentally ill were easily dismissed in the ancient world. Such a ruling would hardly have evoked much dissent. Likewise, can. 80 barring freedmen from the episcopal rank contained no controversial move: freedmen were socially outclassed by the bishops and did not have much of a chance to break that barrier.

However, it was one thing to deal with the insane of can. 29 or with the freedmen of can. 80, who were not serious threats, but quite another to deal with fellow clerics, especially those actually present during the council's proceedings. In cases touching on their concerns, the reason for a canon's omission of a sanction was not the relative unimportance of its topic, but the vested interest of the clergy. Can. 27 is a good example. The sexual dilemma was surely not a side issue for this council; yet when someone brought up the question as to what kind of women should live in a cleric's house, he made the council face a delicate problem. The council did not dare, or at any rate was not willing, to express any kind of punishment for those who would not comply with its ruling. The two decisions of 27 are exceedingly instructive. Compared with all the violent condemnations of sexual conduct, exhibited by the d^4 and d^5 penalties, 27b was quite mild. What would happen if a bishop did not obey? No one in the assembly wanted to come to terms with that delicate problem. No one challenged the sentence. Perhaps some bishops or presbyters had other women living with them; perhaps the synod shrewdly was aware that its demand could not be enforced. In comparison with the rest of the rulings, the d^1 and d^2 decisions of can. 27 are mild.

The relative leniency of the d^2 pattern can be measured by comparing can. 15 with the two subsequent canons. Can. 15, prohibiting marriage between Christian and pagan, was pronounced with less vehemence than can. 16, prohibiting marriage between Christian and Jew or Christian and heretic. In turn, can. 16 was expressed less violently than can. 17, prohibiting marriage between a Christian girl and a pagan priest. Taken by itself, the decision in can. 15 could be understood as extremely strong. In comparison with the two subsequent decision patterns (16 has a d^4 decision and 17 a d^5 decision), it proves to be the weakest of the negations employed by the council.

The character of such a simple negative decision can be read in one piece of evidence in can. 9. Here the council states that a woman may not marry another man after having left her husband. This was a straightforward prohibition. But the canon goes on to say: if she does *(si duxerit)*. This phrase indicates that the kind of prohibition expressed in the first part of the canon is really only a hope, a wish, an ideal. One can not say that the clerics were fully conscious of what they were doing in that canon, nor can one accuse them of making lighthearted decisions. Yet the dilution of the first part of the canon in the second reveals their uncertainty.

If They Do This, We Shall Throw Them Out—d^3

From the simple d^2 prohibition can be distinguished a small group of prohibitions which say more than merely: They must do this, yet which contain neither penance (d^4) nor final exclusion from the community (d^5). Instead, they include a threat in the prohibition: They must not do this or else we shall throw them out. The ambiguity present in Elvira's language is nowhere as obvious as in these threats. They were directed toward two separate goals: exclusion and deposition. The threat of exclusion was flung at laymen: They shall be kept away (34), They shall be anathematized (52); the threat of deposition at clerics: They shall be removed (30), They shall be deposed (51).[21] Whether exclusion or deposition was carried out is entirely beside the point. What is to the point is the fact that the synod had a clear way to express irrevocable exclusion if it meant that: If you do this, you shall not receive communion even on your deathbed.

---

21. One could separate the two aspects of the d^3 pattern, making two distinct patterns out of them, but what is significant is that they both threaten a form of expulsion.

In the d^3 decisions it did not express absolute exclusion from the *communio*.

The d^3 pattern, thus, is a decision that sounds more fierce, more highly charged than d^2. Yet the fact that the synod did not mean or dare to phrase a levy of penance or irrevocable exclusion can imply frustration as well as anger. Can. 52, for instance, prescribes that people who have placed derogatory writings *(libelli famosi)* in churches shall be anathematized. Anathematized even to the end? If so, why did the canon not say that? Would the accused receive communion if he were to die the next day? Was he too important or too unimportant to be disciplined by such heavy ammunition as the threat of the final withholding of communion? One does not know. But it is clear that if the bishops had wanted to threaten him they could have done so. For some reason, the bishops did not want to commit themselves. Surely they were angry at the Spaniard who laughed at them in their churches. Surely they were angrier at him than at those who merely painted on the walls of their sanctuaries. The d^3 decision against satires (52) is more intense in its rage than the d^2 decision against images (36). Yet, their anger is tempered. They could have issued a *nec-in-finem* warning, but the fact that they did not indicates they wanted to leave themselves a loophole.

When directed against the laity, the command "They shall abstain," unsupported by a penitential injunction, was vague, after all. An insane person, can. 37b declares, shall not light candles in church *(d^2);* 37c declares that if he does so anyhow, he shall abstain *(d^3).* But abstain for how long? Permanently? The canon does not specify, and one understands precisely why. Threats of penance or exclusion would not control the mentally ill. Experience had taught the church that hard fact, which is why baptism was granted to the possessed person only on his deathbed. And yet the church understandably would not welcome the participation of such ill persons in the liturgy. The demand to abstain left open what would happen to them.

One could assume that *arceri* (to abstain, to be cut off, to be kept out) was the most extreme pronouncement available to the synod.

Yet, that was not the case, for its use in the d^3 pattern was not necessarily extreme. Can. 78 consists of two decisions on adultery between Christian and Jew or Christian and pagan. Can. 78a declares that if a Christian commits such an act he shall be cut off from the community; can. 78b, however, stipulates that if the adulterer is denounced by an informer, he shall receive five years' penance. The offense of 78b is beyond doubt worse in the eyes of the clerics. The purpose of so phrasing the canon was to encourage transgressors who had not confessed their sin into confessing, so that 78a would apply. What does 78a mean, then, in saying that a person is cut off from the community? Clearly, this sanction was meant to be less severe than five years' penance. How much less severe? Could the penalty have been three years' penance? That would have been rather lenient in the value scale of the council.[22] Four years' penance is unlikely since nowhere in the canons does the council operate with a four-year scheme. But such speculations are irrelevant. The point is that the *arceatur* of 78a is an expression of disapproval which remained unspecified but which certainly did not imply an extreme disciplinary measure.

The same relatively mild force of the arceatur is revealed in can. 34: a believer lighting candles in a cemetery in the daytime shall be cut off from the church.[23] Lighting candles in cemeteries was a vestige of pagan rites. Although the synod chose only one aspect of the custom, namely lighting candles in the daytime, even of that custom it chose not to make an important issue. Why not? Perhaps the candlelighters themselves were too unimportant, or conversely, too significant. Perhaps the practice was so widespread the synod could not have enforced strong disciplinary measures with any amount of success. The canon, in any case, was really an expression of irritation or resistance to customs that represented what was either not yet, or no longer, a major issue.

When directed against the clergy, the d^3 pattern always had

---

22. Hefele, vol. 1, p. 262, deals with the problem of arceri in can. 78 (see also Dale, *Elvira and Christian Life,* p. 96). Similarly indeterminate is the abstineatur of 74.

23. Joseph Jungmann, *La liturgie des premiers siècles* (Paris, 1962), p. 278.

stronger and more specific sanctions than when directed against lay-men: a cleric is commanded to abstain from his wife and not to beget children; otherwise he shall be deposed (33). However, even this sanction does not represent the strongest measure available. While can. 33 threatened the married clergy with deposition (d^3), can. 18, dealing with adultery committed by clerics, threatened the transgressors with irrevocable exclusion (d^5). Since adultery certainly was regarded as the stronger sin, the d^5 pattern is more severe than the d^3. Similarly, the threat of deposition against subdeacons who had committed fornication in their youth (30), expressed in the d^3 patterns, was less severe than the threat in can. 18. In summary, the d^3 decisions, in their various degrees of severity, show again that a synodal No was not a simple, clear prohibition. When compared to the d^5 sentences, the tentativeness and the indeterminateness of the d^3 decisions become obvious.

If They Do This, They Must Do Penance—d^4

The fourth decision pattern is the penitential one: If they do this, they shall abstain. Although *abstinere*, a major term expressing exclusion from the community, appears seventeen times, only twenty-seven of 134 decisions specify a particular length of time for penance. Only in one-fifth of all the cases before it did the synod impose a temporal period of penance on its culprits. Such discipline was applied against both catechumens and baptized Christians; termination of discipline meant for the first group admittance to baptism and for the second readmittance to communion. A survey of the entire scale of penance discloses with what amazingly capricious measures this synod operated.

A short time *(pauco tempore)* of abstention was imposed on a person who missed church three times (21). Such was the most lenient penance exacted by the assembly. The canon does not specify how long "a short time" is to be. One suspects that it meant a few weeks, perhaps a few months. It would seem that it had to be less

· 41 ·

than one year, since missing church three times surely was not as grave a crime, even· for so unpredictable a synod, as the transgressions which are punished by a one-year penance.

A *one-year* exclusion from the Christian community was pronounced in a few cases: in one instance, against a Christian girl who slept with a man before marriage but who married him afterwards (14),[24] and, in another, against a person who played dice (79). A period of one year's exclusion can also be inferred from can. 56. When a Christian was elected to the office of *duumvir,* he had to abstain from the Christian communion for that year, since during the year of his office he had to participate in objectionable public events, above all in sacrifices.

A *two-yea*r sentence was passed in two cases: first, against a priest who wore a crown yet who had not sacrificed nor made a contribution to idols (55); and second, against a false witness who could demonstrate that he had committed his crime with hesitation (74). Also, a two-year period of discipline was required as the normal catechumenate (42).

A *three-year* period was imposed in several cases: against flamines who became catechumens and did not sacrifice during that period (4), against parents who broke the vow of betrothal (54), against persons lending clothes to a participant in a pagan parade (57), and against a deacon who had committed a mortal sin and yet who had himself ordained, provided he, and not someone else, revealed that sin (76).

A *five-year* penance was applied in no fewer than twelve canons: against the mistress who beat a girl slave to death, provided she did it accidentally (5); against a woman catechumen who married a man who had left his innocent wife (11);[25] against a girl who had slept not with one but with more than one man (14); against parents who gave their daughter either to a heretic or to a Jew (16); against landholders who accepted as rent goods which had been offered to idols

24. The only canon pronouncing exclusion sine poenitentia is 14.
25. The catechumena of can. 11 is the same as the one in can. 10b.

(40); against a man who had married his sister-in-law (61); against a man who had committed adultery once (69); against an informer, provided he was a catechumen or provided his information did not lead to proscription or death (73); against a false witness who could not prove his innocence (74); against a deacon who did not confess his transgression himself, but was reported by someone else (76); against a Christian who had committed adultery with a Jew or a pagan (78); against a widow who had sexual relations with a man whom she afterwards married (72).

A *seven-year* sentence was pronounced once, against the woman who had flogged her slave so harshly that the victim died within three days (5). While she would have received a five-year sentence if she had killed the girl accidentally, she was given seven years for doing so on purpose *(voluntate)*.

A *ten-year* sentence appeared in six canons: against a Catholic who had gone over to heresy (22); against a Christian who had not come to church for a long time, provided he had not sacrificed during that period (46); against a Christian who had ascended to the Capitol of a town during the time sacrifices were performed there (59); against a man who knew his wife had committed adultery, continued to live with her, yet finally left her (70); against a man who married an adulterous widow (72).

Is penance identical with exclusion? The canons seem to say so, although there is a certain ambiguity typical of ancient Christianity's legal and ethical language: some canons add penance to exclusion, while others do not. One canon (14a) explicitly pronounces exclusion without penance *(sine poenitentia)*.[26] However, that canon, de-

---

26. There are four types of penitential canons distinct from the anathema-deposition pattern of d^3 and from the nec in finem pattern of d^5: 1—canons demanding a period of exclusion without specifically naming penance (4, 11, 14, 16, 40, 46, 54, 55, 56, 61, 69, 73, 74, 79); 2—canons demanding a period of exclusion and specifically naming penance (5, 22, 59, 64, 72, 76, 78); 3—canons speaking about exclusion sine poenitentia (14a only); 4—canons speaking about penance without naming a period of exclusion (3, 7, 13, 31). The first two types are analogous; *post tempora constituta* and *acta poenitentia* are side by side in can. 7. The first type implies the same sort of penance expressed in the second, with the exception of 56. Hence, exclusion and penance are concomitants except in very few cases: 14a, which enjoins against penance;

claring an exclusion of one year, and perhaps also can. 56, are the only ones expressing a period of exclusion without penance. Both dictate only one-year exclusions, and therefore deal with mild cases. Can. 14, which expressly enjoins against penance, is therefore certainly not typical. The many other sentences of exclusion which do not mention poenitentia nevertheless imply it, in my view, since they contain little substantive variation. The canons which do mention penance are in the beginning of the synod (3, 5, 13, 14) or toward the end (59, 64, 69, 72, 76, 78), with only three exceptions (22, 31, 32). I deduce from this fact that particular bishops phrasing particular sententiae wanted to emphasize that exclusion was at the same time penance; hence, they were explicit. Perhaps they wanted to be so because they were used to such phraseology, or else because exclusion did not necessarily mean penance in all churches. The possibility is supported by the significant fact that the stringent nec in finem phrase clusters similarly, appearing in the first eighteen and in the last nineteen canons. The observer must consider the possibility that the men who phrased the first and the last canons of that synod came from churches that had an especially rigoristic disciplinary tradition and practice.[27]

Such are the d^4 decisions made by the synod. Even a cursory reading of the material proves the point made earlier that these decisions were not planned systematically, but arose from spontaneous reactions to individual cases that were brought up. These reactions varied greatly: a woman who killed a slave received a penance of five or seven years (5), while a person not going to church for some time (46) or going to the temple of the Capitoline Jupiter or Capitoline

---

56, which cannot have put the duumvir under penitential discipline; 3 and 13, which join penance to deathbed mercy; 31, which levies penance without specifying exclusion. Can. 32 deals merely with penitential procedures.

27. The canons expressing a period of penance are among the first 16 or the last 28 canons of the corpus, beginning with can. 54. Of the 37 canons between 16 and 54, only three pronounce a period of discipline: 22, 40, and 46. Can. 31 does not deal with the length of penance. I believe these facts indicate first that to some bishops of the council the practice of specifying penance by a definite period of time was more familiar than to others, and second that the penitential system, for which Elvira is so famous, was not fixed, but rather only coming into being, and therefore operable only part of the time.

Trinity at the forum (59) received ten years. The canons do not elucidate exactly what was meant by the penitential discipline, but they could not have proclaimed exclusion merely from eucharistic service. In that communio in the ancient church was a much more inclusive term, designating the church as a social and theological, as well as liturgical, body, exclusion from that communion meant that an individual was cut off from that body.

The question has to be raised, of course, whether such exclusion was actually practiced as stated. The second and third decision patterns have made it clear that the phrasing of an ethical command did not necessarily mean the intention was carried out, and that legal language expressed not only coercion but threat, anger, hope, and irresolution. The same possibility of distinction between intent and actual enforcement must be considered in the canons on penance.[28] Several observations strongly justify such distinctions. In the first place, the penitential canons are exceedingly vaccilating; their measures of discipline change from five to seven, from two to seven, from ten to five and back to ten years without necessarily a consistent correlation between the sin and the duration of penance. The arbitrariness of such terms implies an astonishing degree of manipulation of a believer's life on the part of the church. The lack of correlation between punishment and crime suggests also that the sentences were not necessarily executed precisely as they were passed. A five-year sentence might have been commuted to four or three years, or even fewer.[29] In the second place, the penitential decisions are at times so tentative, and so often are juxtaposed to d^2 and d^3 decisions that they certainly can not be regarded as parts of a carefully wrought penitential system. They were more like scattershot efforts to coerce the flock into submission. In the third place, like the ancient church, which gives us many examples proving how easily seemingly harsh and angry

---

28. Cans. 9, 72. The problem goes back to the earliest church. Paul anathematized a man in 1 Cor. 5:5. In 2 Cor. 2:7 he appealed for clemency. We do not know if both expressions apply to the same case but the plea shows the vacillating patterns in Paul.

29. Good illustrations of the arbitrariness of the canonic decisions are 2–4, 9, 55–60, 72, 78. Can. 54 vacillates between blaming and excusing the parents.

pronouncements could be forgotten, Elvira should not be accepted at face value.[30] Public penance, which the synod of Elvira tried to set up, was soon replaced at least partially by private penance.[31] All these indications point to a wide gap between penitential theory and penitential enforcement. Local discipline with its face-to-face interrelations was different from the lofty jurisdictional process carried on in an ecclesiastical basilica.

If They Do This, There Shall Be No Mercy Even at the End—d⁵

The most extreme of the penitential measures is irrevocable exclusion: If they do this, there shall be no mercy even at the end. Eighteen canons state expressly, and two imply, that certain sinners are not to be taken back into the communion of the church at all, not even at the end of their lives, on their deathbeds (nec in finem).[32] These decisions are separated here into a special pattern because they do not mete out penance proper, but total anathema. It makes quite a difference—for the person on the receiving end—whether he is sentenced to temporary exclusion, even a prolonged one, or thrown out for good. In these nec in finem decisions ancient Christianity fired its strongest ammunition. These twenty d^5 cases represent fascinating examples of a highly emotional language pattern that has proved effective into the twentieth century. I shall examine in a later chapter the cultural and psychological conditions which permitted the Christian church to get away with such threats. The s^1 and s^2 segments

---

30. Nicaea, cans. 11, 12. Samuel Laeuchli, *The Serpent and the Dove* (New York, 1966), p. 189. fn. 84.

31. R. C. Mortimer, *The Origins of Private Penance in the Western Church* (Oxford, 1939).

32. In can. 3b the decision *ulterius hi non esse dandam communionem* is a reversal of the in finem decision in 3a, and therefore implies a nec in finem sanction; in can. 47b, likewise, the decision reverses the earlier decision of 47a, which granted communion in fine mortis. To be sure, by not expressing nec in finem in 47b, the synod may have left a door open for reconciliation. It is more likely, however, that the man phrasing the sententia of 47 was not familiar with the nec in finem phrase as other bishops were.

which name Christians condemned by the synod with the threat of irrevocable exclusion are:

1: a man who goes to a temple as idolater
2: a flamen who falls back after baptism
3: a flamen who falls back into sexual sin after penance (the nec in finem is implied)
6: a person practicing witchcraft and killing someone thereby
7: a person committing fornication after having already undergone penance for such an act
8: a woman leaving her husband without any cause
12: parents who give their children into prostitution
13: dedicated virgins who break their vows
17: parents who give their daughter into marriage to a pagan priest
18: bishops, presbyters, and deacons committing a sexual sin
47: a man who commits adultery after repentance (the canon implies nec in finem)
63: a woman undergoing abortion
64: a woman living to the end of her life with a man not her husband
65: priests who do not throw out their adulterous wives
66: people who marry their mothers-in-law
70: husbands who know their wives committed adultery and who continue to live with them
71: homosexuals
72: a widow who sleeps with one man and marries another
73: informers whose information leads to proscription and death
75: people who bring charges against bishops and presbyters without proving their cases

Curiously, the d^5 decisions are found primarily at the beginning and toward the end of the council's deliberations. The high points of emotion during the proceedings of the synod were reached in the first eighteen and in the last nineteen canons.[33]

33. The step from d^4 to d^5 is the step from Sardica, can. 1 to can. 2. I can not accept Gaudemet's view, in *L'Eglise dans l'Empire Romain, IVe et Ve siècles* (Paris, 1958) p. 72, that the nec in finem anathemata "n'implique que l'exclusion des sacrements." See also Gaudemet's "Note sure les formes anciennes de l'excommunication," *Rev. des Sciences Rel.* 36 (1949):64ff. Communio at the beginning of the fourth century en-

The topics of these d^5 decisions reveal where the clerics' crucial problems lay. Basically, they were still the three capital sins of the primitive church: murder, apostasy and adultery.[34] However, murder was dealt with rarely by the church: it is ancillary to can. 6 and it is part of can. 73. More crucial problems were idolatry and sex. Five canons deal with idolatry (1, 2, 3, 17, 73). Fifteen canons deal with sexual problems, which included not only matters of marriage, adultery, and divorce, but also of homosexuality, abortion, and other transgressions against the sexual code of the church. Three canons deal with the hierarchy (18, 65, 75). Later sections will deal with these two key problems of the church as they emerge from the d^5 decisions: the elite position of the clergy and the sexual taboos of the church.

Under the Pressure of Illness, There Shall Be Mercy on Their Deathbed—d^6

The last decision pattern qualifies the punishment meted out by the d^4 and d^5 patterns: Under the pressure of illness—or in the face of death—mercy shall be offered. If a catechumen who had been given a five-year penance fell terribly ill, the sentence was to be lifted and baptism was to be granted (11). Such a declaration of mercy differed in kind from the straightforward affirmations expressed in the d^4 pattern: it was exclusively deathbed forgiveness, mercy at the end, in fine (10, 68), *in fine mortis* (37). In the case of a catechumen, forgiveness meant acceptance for baptism (11); in the case of a baptized Christian, the granting of communion (37).[35] The synod reversed

---

compassed more than merely the liturgical communion (Dale, p. 94). In the use of the d^5 pattern the synod dealt its strongest blow. Dale gives two lists of extreme condemnations, one with 24 canons (p. 95, fn. 7) and one with 5 (p. 96, fn. 9), totalling 29. My analysis puts canons 20, 30, 33, 34, 37, 41, 49, and 51 of his list into other categories.

34. Tertullian *De Pud*. 1ff.

35. The phrase "baptismum placuit non denegari" is the reluctant phrase of clemency in 11. On the difference between the punishment of catechumens and baptized see Dale pp. 87–88, 112–13.

penitential sentences of five (61), seven (5), and even ten years (72), and made exceptions from total exclusion (13). The most striking phrase is *necessitas infirmitatis*. "Under the pressure of illness" certain persons were to receive communion (1, 38, 61, 69). Apparently, such mercy did not come naturally or freely; illness "forced" (*coegerit,* 72) the reversal of a penitential sanction.

To speak about necessity of illness is a strange way to express a rationale for clemency. Why would sickness coerce mercy upon a church? The phrase suggests man's fear of death: in the face of grave sickness he tends to become considerably softer and more forgiving. In the d^6 decisions the clerics acted in their priestly function. When they granted mercy because of the pressure of illness, they said in fact: We give you mercy because death is such a serious business and because our priestly duty necessitates mercy; it is our metier to forgive, though we do it reluctantly. The more sparingly and unwillingly they granted mercy to the sinners, the more grateful these sinners were going to be for it. These decisions were granted sparingly indeed. Of fifty strict, punitive measures (d^4 and d^5), only seventeen cases of mercy were granted. Against 101 negative decisions (d^2 through d^5), there are only seventeen decisions of clemency, so strongly did negation prevail over mercy.

On what grounds were such exemptions made? It is hard to tell. The seventeen d^6 decisions do not exhibit a great deal of logical consistency. The granting of deathbed forgiveness seems to have depended less on the accused or the crime than on the momentary mood of the synod, or of individuals in the synod, at a given moment of the proceedings. The mercy clause was offered to catechumens (38), widows (72), men (10) as well as women (11), dedicated virgins (13), and the mentally ill (37). There is some consistency, however, for the mercy clause is offered only once on grounds other than proximity of death or illness (54), and it is never offered to the clergy.[36] Furthermore, it is offered more readily to the unbaptized than to the

---

36. Dale, p. 82.

faithful. The crime of abortion, for instance, draws a severe d^5 decision against a baptized woman (63), and a d^6 against a catechumen (68). Such differentiation established the baptized as privileged, but also as subject therefore to stricter regulations by the clergy. In differentiating between d^5 and d^6, the synod strengthened the arcane character of the church.

Only when taken as isolated units do the patterns seem clear and straightforward; complexities emerge as soon as one holds one pattern against the others. In the evaluation of the differences among them lies the key to an understanding of the canons. It was not simply a question of the synod's choosing between d^1 and d^5: conform or we throw you out! If one had asked one of the bishops present at the council, he might have said that of course he was making just that choice. This analysis shows that his answer would have been wrong. The utopian dream of clear moral choices did not correspond to the experience in the daily life of the patristic age any more than it does in our own. The subtle discriminations in the patterns prove that it was impossible for the synod to make simplistic responses to the conflicts confronting it.

One can see the importance of nuances of differences in the patterns of those canons that cope with the fact of impending death: in fine versus nec in finem. To offer an alternative to extinction was one of the major theological tasks of the ancient world. One sect after another offered rebirth, eternal life, immortality, or resurrection in one form or another. The extraordinary fear of death and the desperate hope for afterlife were not related exclusively to the exceedingly high mortality resulting from bacteriological infection. Such tangible, imminent threats to life always have been present in human existence. What accounts for the religious quest in the age of the Roman Empire was the additional factor of a new consciousness of and sensitivity to the imminence and inevitability of death. As man began to experience the emergence of his individuality, he gradually began to develop a different attitude toward his precarious situation in life. He began to resist the inevitability of the natural cycle with its agony. He fought back by countering his fear with images of re-birth and immortality. Through the deathbed decision pattern the church appealed to such heightened sensitivity and used it to estab-lish clerical supremacy. The threat to refuse mercy—the threat of eternal damnation—was the strongest weapon the church ever pos-sessed for enforcing social control. Down to Voltaire who, despite his atheism and vituperative attacks on the church, accepted extreme unction, the deathbed threat was the Damoclean sword over the lives of the baptized. Anyone who has lived in a town where such threats still have some power knows of the panic which can be aroused by the refusal of the priest to perform the traditional rites associated with death and dying, when the victim is an apostate, a suicide, or a part-ner in a mixed marriage.

Considering such a fear of death in ancient man, one realizes that it mattered very much whether a decision was made in a d^5 or d^6 pat-tern. The two are opposites: one throws the accused deeper into his fear of death, the other saves him from it, at least temporarily. By choosing between d^5 and d^6 the clerics exercised, in effect, a life and death power; they played on the deepest emotions in the tormented lives of their contemporaries. Yet, the synod did not seem totally aware of its responsibility in making its choices. The cases in which mercy was promised surely were not arrived at carefully, but resulted from spontaneous reactions in the procedural drama. Since the dis-tinction between d^5 and d^6 was such a crucial one, yet was often made so arbitrarily, one is inclined to wonder how the Christian church dared to play so carelessly with the fears of its believers? The answer lies in the fact that damnation and mercy can be children of the same parents, and that they can serve the same purpose: to tighten clerical domination in the church. The clerics decided whom to damn and whom to excuse, but which way they ruled mattered less than the fact that the synod took upon itself the privilege and power to make life and death choices. It is in the making of such choices that the clergy gained maneuverability, and solidified its power as it struggled to establish itself.

Alternations of patterns occur frequently in the same canon. While 13a presents a d^5 decision, 13b presents a d^6. Can. 3a moves from d^6 to the d^5 decision of 3b, just as 47a moves from d^6 to the d^5 decision of 47b. Such alternation of patterns, however, takes place not from d^5 to d^6 decisions, but involves other combinations as well. Almost half of the entire corpus of Elvira, thirty-seven canons, present mixed rather than single decisions. I list a few examples to show the range of combinations:

d^1, d^2: 27, 53
d^2, d^4: 16, 57, 74
d^3, d^4: 78, 79
d^4, d^6: 32, 61, 69
d^5, d^4: 64, 70

Certain canons display three or even four different emotional patterns. In the three parts of can. 9, we find d^2, d^4, and d^6 decisions. In the four parts of 72, d^4, d^5, d^4, and d^6.

Such are the rhythms and decision patterns in the canons of Elvira. The task has been to find a way through the labyrinth of these peculiar, often conflicting sentences in order to discover how the synod came to its decisions. To explain the differences between decisions one has to try to read the mind of the synod by analyzing what it says. This process leads to important insights into the penitential, conciliar, and ethical language of the ancient church. In the first place one can not take it for granted that prohibitory statements in ancient Christian texts were carried out eo ipso.[37] The opposite may often have been the case. Let us suppose that by some coincidence only the

---

37. A good example is the phraseology of 9: "foemina quae ducit . . . prohibeatur ne ducat; si duxerit. . . ." Gams (vol. 2, pp. 28ff.) saw long ago that the decision of a canon might not have been carried out as stated. Dale's polemic (pp. 99–100) misses the point. Neither the lack of external evidence that sentences were not carried out, nor the reiteration by later councils of certain strict measures of Elvira, proves that they were carried out, or that they were always carried out as stated. The differences in the language patterns of d^2, d^3, and d^5 show that we cannot naively assume that texts necessarily mean what they literally say, any more than we naively accept, to use my example, President Nixon's claim to be pro-peace, ipso facto.

d^2 and d^3 decisions of Elvira had come down to our time. One would have assumed naively that these sentences were meant to be carried out: a man was condemned to be excluded from the church and was thrown out. Yet, a comparison of patterns has revealed that even simple prohibitions could express complicated emotional attitudes or political purpose rather than a simple determination to enforce a point at issue. This is not to imply that in every ethical or conciliar text of the ancient church a straightforward prohibition is necessarily suspect, but one has to be exceedingly cautious before drawing an apparently obvious conclusion from a prohibitive phrase. Language often does lie, and this realization is crucial for understanding secular as well as religious texts. Take the problem of Rome's persecution of Christians. If language were to be taken at face value, either Rome would have enforced its edicts and murdered virtually hundreds of thousands of Christians, leaving the churches emptied of adult believers, or the church would have had to throw out a similar number of apostates, reducing its flock to an extremely small church of the martyrs. Neither was the case. The d^2 and d^3 patterns of these canons make it clear why this was not so: an anathema spoken does not always mean an anathema carried out.

In the second place, the analysis has shown that one can measure the degree to which the synod meant, or did not mean, to enforce a specific anathema. There is a certain method behind the inconsistencies of Elvira. When the synod chose a pattern, it also chose whether it was willing to test its authority on the case or not. After all, the ancient church did throw out some of its members as scapegoats for the community, and it was responsible for producing one schism after another. One must learn, therefore, not only to understand the arbitrariness in the language of coercion, but to distinguish the anathema of pure threat from the anathema that was meant to be carried out, whether or not it actually was carried out in every instance. How important the choice of a decision pattern was can be shown in the way the synod dealt with its clergy. As has been pointed out, the council never allowed d^6, the deathbed clemency, to a cleric. Was the council, then, excessively strict toward its own members? Not always. When it did not see a way to enforce its decision on the clergy, it chose the simple prohibition of the d^2 pattern, which left the matter open. When it came to disciplining the clergy, therefore, the crucial choice was made not at the point of granting or not granting final mercy (choosing between d^5 and d^6), but at the point of choosing a decision pattern that either assumed or tacitly denied the chance of success (choosing between d^5 and d^2).[38] Of course, not every d^5 anathema was necessarily carried out. We can no longer check the results.

In the third place, the intertwining of decision patterns reveals the social dilemma of this council, and behind it, of the church entering upon the age of imperial Christianity. Dogmatism and uncertainty, a willingness to be inclusive concomitant with an arrogant exclusivity, and underlying all, the drive to dominate and the desire to act as priest—all these emotions tore at the leaders who assembled in the southern Spanish town.[39] What was their church? In what lay its identity? One can not say absolutely. The clerics themselves did not know. And the evidences they left behind are incomplete and ambiguous. This church contained Montanist, Catholic, imperial, and provincial elements. The canons passed on by the men who travelled to Illiberis give no clear result; instead, they hint at a drama. By try-

38. There were, therefore, not only two ways to deal with the clergy, namely deposition (E. Vacanard, "La déposition des évêques," *Revue du clergé français*, 54 [1908]:388) and excommunication (Hess, *Council of Sardica*, p. 79), but three: deposition, threat of excommunication, and excommunication. Cans. 20, 30, and 33 are certainly deposition threats, but 19, 27, 50, and 53 are not. Can. 53 is a border case, actually, in that it threatens the offenders rather strongly (*status sui periculo*) although the threat is not expressed concretely; different from 18, it does not express deposition. The canon which best shows the tentativeness of the canonic language against the clergy is 19.

39. The complex decision patterns point to a tense internal situation in Spain. What really went on is of course beyond recovery; but Augustine's enigmatic phrase "Ossius ab Hispania damnatus a Gallis absolutus" (*Epist. contra Parmenidem* 1.47) may contain the remembrance of deep cleavages in Spanish Christianity in the early fourth century. In the Priscillian schism later on in the century, the Christian churches of the peninsula revealed deep social cleavages (V. C. de Clercq, "Ossius of Cordova and the Origins of Priscillianism," *Studia Patristica* [1957], 1:601–606).

ing to recreate that drama, one learns in what directions fourth-century Christianity was heading. In succeeding pages I shall analyze what I believe were the central preoccupations of the council, namely, the establishment of clerical identity and of sexual control.

Three

THE STRUGGLE FOR IDENTITY

For centuries the conflict with the Roman Empire had played a key role in giving the Christian church its identity: Christ was Kyrios, not Caesar. The public sacrificial ceremony was the locus which the church chose in order to mark its separation from the larger cultural context. "We do not sacrifice to Caesar" meant in fact: "We are a special community; our models of salvation, our Kyrios, are better than the empire's." No matter how often the church's ideological recalcitrance led to martyrdom and how often it was de facto ignored by tacit acquiescence to Roman pressures, the dichotomy worked because church discipline could be enforced. Christians were set apart. However, as Christianity moved into a new age in which the conflict between the church and the empire began to dwindle, the concrete value of the ideological polemic decreased. What then defined a Christian church in its *civitas* and province once it became a majority religion? The canons of Elvira are an excellent document for examining how the church redefined itself, how it moved, by an intricate semi-intuitive process, toward the Constantinian solution, how it tried out playing the role of a major cultural force, and how in that transition primitive Christian anticultural forces collided with the new pro-Roman forces. Above all, the canons demonstrate that it was the Christian clergy that pushed the church into the new epoch.[1]

1. It is surprising that de Clercq could protest against Dale: "Among the eighty-one canons, there is no suggestion for the development of a sacerdotal class" (p. 113). As Dale saw clearly, there is a good deal of evidence for such development.

THE NEW ELITE

In the canons of Elvira a group of bishops and presbyters, acting as a new provincial elite, heaped threat upon threat on all sorts of people in the Christian fold. Did these threats work? We do not know. Were they actually carried out? We do not know that either. Yet, we can analyze these threats, this intricate jigsaw puzzle of command, anathema, and penalty along with an occasional offer of mercy. In the variations of these threats one can measure almost seismographically the intensity and range of a momentous struggle which these clerics waged in order to secure the victory of the church over its external forces and in order to tighten their rein over that church.[2] In fighting for these two goals simultaneously the bishops and presbyters inevitably intertwined the issue of idolatry with that of clerical hierarchy.

In respect to the first of these struggles, the canons reveal an amazing ambivalence in the decisions taken by the council. One senses its determination to fight the imperial cultic elite of the age, but one also feels its desire to function precisely like a Roman assembly. A flamen, for instance, was judged by a most severe code, while a duumvir was judged by a lenient code. This disparity, on examination, is not as arbitrary as it appears. It belongs to the transitional age in which Christianity, half afraid still of the empire's brutality and unsure of its own potential, pushed forward and actually prepared itself for the arrival of the *aureum saeculum,* the triumph of the church.

In respect to the second struggle, that within the church, the canons prove how exceedingly complex the task of controlling the Christian fold turned out to be. It was relatively simple and it sounded brave to hurl passionate threats against the converted, even though they had been upper-class priests of the imperial cult. It might well be that in these cases the threats worked well. After all, the self-conscious desire of the convert to please makes him easily amenable to discipline. But

---

2. The clerical leadership exhibited what Richard M. Honig called Wille zum Neuaufbau (*Humanitas und Rhetorik in spätrömischen Kaisergesetzen* [Göttingen, 1960], p. 7).

to hurl threats against other important members of the church—
women living in luxury, holders of estates, clerics involved in finan-
cial affairs—turned out to be much less efficacious. From the uncertain character of many of these threats one can conclude that the
synod felt much constraint in its attempts to control its own rich and
powerful. Yet the synod tried. In these attempts, no matter how frequently they vacillated between anger and compromise, the process
can be traced by which the Christian clergy began to play the role of
a new cultic elite in the Roman Empire.

First, we can investigate certain canons which express aspects of
the relationship between the Christian hierarchy and the imperial
power structure. A first group contains the opening canons 1 through
4, in which apostate Christians (1) and apostate former priests of
pagan imperial religion (2–4) are dealt with severely. It has been
established that the synod displayed in its units of decision a variety
of emotional charges, designated d^1 through d^6, the most severe being
d^5 (nec in finem). The first four canons, which actually contain five
decisions, exemplify the emotional range with a remarkable emphasis on d^5. Cans. 1, 2, and 3b contain d^5 decisions. Given this sequence,
one would conclude that the synod opened in a state of excitement.
While in the overall mood of the council only one out of every six
decisions was of the d^5 degree, in this group of canons three out of
five were of such order. The synod reached this kind of anger again
only much later, in the series on anathemata, beginning with can. 63.
Idolatrous behavior and, above all, the apostasy of former flamines,
were therefore extremely serious matters as the synod began its
deliberations.

A second group (15–17) demonstrates how serious a threat idolatry seemed to the clergy. The three canons pronounce various levies
for what was actually the same transgression, namely the case of a
Christian girl's marriage to some non-Christian man. Yet the degree
of punishment increases from one canon to the next. The marriage
between a Christian girl and an average pagan man elicits a d^2 sentence in can. 15, while the marriage between a Christian girl and a

heretic or a Jew produces a d^4 two-year sentence in can. 16. The marriage between a Christian girl and a pagan priest, however, was punished by d^5 in can. 17. In this progression from d^2 to d^4 to d^5 we feel the synod's rising anger, climaxing in the decision against Christians who dared to affiliate with the pagan priesthood.

The synod opened its session by facing the traditional matter of idolatry. However, as case after case was brought up and deliberations went on, other issues pushed the whole matter of idolatry into the background.[3] The problem did return in a group of canons in which the church's conflicts with priests (55), magistrates (56), people who went to sacrifices (59), and people who broke pagan idols (60) were expressed. The decisions made in 55–60 reveal that the council's attitude toward the established power structure of the day had changed. Cans. 55, 56, 57, and 59 all contain d^4 decisions, of two, one, three, and 10 years, respectively; 58 and 60 contain d^2 decisions. There is a distinct difference between the punishment scale of cans. 55–60 and that of 1–4. There is not one d^5 measure in the 55–60 group. The d^4 sentences are mild, and, although can. 59 is rather strict, it is followed immediately by the conciliatory tone of can. 60. The synod, adopting a more tolerant attitude toward pagan culture, certainly was in a much less punitive or hostile mood when it passed on the cases of cans. 55–60 than it was when it opened its proceedings. This mood is the more striking in contrast with the rigor expressed in cans. 63–72 dealing with sexual deviations.[4] In cans. 55–60 the traditional struggle with the religious pagan powers (55, 57, 59) was giving way to a struggle on the part of the church to establish itself as a major force in the empire (56, 58, 60).

In two cases (73, 75) we can see how the interest of the synod in the issue of idolatry became connected with the interest in protecting

---

3. This inference results from the assumption that the sequence of procedures in the synod was preserved in the canons. However, the inference also rests on the two tables which demonstrate the secondary place of idolatry in the overall scheme of the synod.

4. Cans. 63–75 represent the largest accumulation of d^5 decisions in the entire synod.

its hierarchical structure. In 73 the force of.the synod was directed against Christians who betrayed their own kind, and in 75 against those who incriminated their own clergy without cause. While can. 73 makes more sense if we assume some violent actions against the church, during which Christians were, through denunciation, proscribed or killed, 75 can be understood easily without assuming an age of persecution prior to the council, since it emulates the practice of Roman law which had always protected its ruling classes, its masters and patrons, against informers.[5] While 73 still reckons with the problem of idolatry, 75 is addressed to the protection of clerical authority. The proximity of these two canons, their parallels and their differences, indicates that the issue of idolatry was related closely to that of ecclesiastical hierarchy; bringing up one could lead quite naturally to a consideration of the other.

The council's positions can be shown by two comparative tables, the first (table 3) showing the distribution of d^5 decisions, and the second (table 4) comparing the frequency of major topics in the overall scheme of the canons. Judging from these severe anathemata, the traditional capital sins of the patristic church—murder, apostasy, and adultery—were still regarded as such by the council of Elvira.[6] However, two significant changes can be observed. In the first place, sexual conduct became a primary issue in the legislation of the council. In the second place, the matter of idolatry did not have the preeminence which it had had in the preceding century. It was ceasing to be the number one issue for a Christian. To be sure, idolatry and hierarchy taken together comprised almost one-third of the d^5 decisions passed by the synod. The struggle to secure clerical control, however, focused less and less on the external enemy, the imperial cult, as the clergy began to center on internal issues. The clergy no longer controlled its

5. *CIL* 3. 12043; Paulus *Opin.* 5.22ff. The laws against informers were extremely cruel (Cicero *De Off.* 2.14; Quintilian, *Inst. Orat.* IV.1.7; XII.7.1–3). The church had used these laws to protect itself in times of persecution, *Act. Procons. Cypr.* 1. The edict of Constantine found in Lyttos in Crete shows how much protection of the hierarchic order was a major concern in the laws against informers (Margarita Guarducci, *Inscriptiones creticae,* vol. 1 [Rome, 1935], pp. 226–27). Cf. Arles, can. 15.

6. Tertullian *De Pud.* 2ff.

TABLE 3

DISTRIBUTION OF d^5 DECISIONS

Topic	Number of Canons	Canons
Murder	2	6, 73
Idolatry	5	1, 2, 3, 6, 73
Hierarchy	3	8, 65, 75
Sexual conduct	15	3, 7, 8, 12, 13, 17, 18, 47, 63, 64, 65, 66, 70, 71, 72

NOTE: Four canons, namely 3, 8, 65, and 73, appear twice in the list because they deal with two major issues.

TABLE 4

FREQUENCY OF ISSUES IN THE CANONS

Issue	Frequency	Percentage
Conflict with Jews or heretics	6	7.4
Idolatry	10	12.4
Hierarchical order	15	18.5
Liturgy, baptism	15	18.5
Economic problems	15	18.5
Pagan culture	18	22.5
Canons directed against or toward women	22	27.2
Canons dealing with sex	37	45.7

NOTE: Many canons deal with several issues. The percentage is given in relation to eighty-one canons.

I include in the category "Canons dealing with sex" only those that legislate explicitly about sexual matters. From a psychological viewpoint, many more canons can be seen to be related to sex. The conflict with the pantomimes, for instance, had sexual undertones, since the pantomimic acts frequently had an overt sexual character (Juvenal *Sat.* 6.63ff.; Suetonius *Dom.* 3; Tacitus *Ann.* 13.20ff.).

subordinates primarily by means of the external conflicts with imperial ideology, but by controlling the sexual behavior of believers. The clerics who assembled at Elvira no longer played the strongly sectarian role of revolutionaries against imperial culture. They no longer were representing persecuted minorities. Their life style, their religious-social dynamic, was encroaching more and more upon the daily secular life of their provinces. The Constantinian age was dawning.

BISHOPS VERSUS CONVERTS
FROM THE FLAMINATE

The manner in which the episcopal and presbyterial assembly of Elvira was operating in strengthening its hold on the church can be observed in the first four canons of the council. When the clerics fought against idolatry, they defended not only the church's ideological claim, but also their own elite status. Can. 1 condemned the *idololaturus,* the Christian believer who committed the crime (*crimen capitale* and *summum scelus*) of apostasy. This canon restates what the patristic church theoretically had always maintained: in regard to the sin of idolatry there can be no compromise.[7] Hence, we have d^5. It is surprising, therefore, to find in can. 2 the same threat hurled against flamines, Christian flamines, that is. Obviously, this canon is unnecessary. If can. 1 had been observed, the flamines would have been included in the anathema and the council would not have needed a second canon to deal specially with them. One can see from these two canons the gap in patristic legislation between demanding and exacting, and the tensions in the churches between ethics and discipline. Either the synod felt that flamines were not threatened enough by can. 1, and added can. 2, or they set up can. 1 as the general platform from which they intended to hit, in the next decision, the former imperial priests, to keep them in line, as it were. In either case, the logically superfluous can. 2 is significant and gives us the clue to the council's intent at its opening session. The climax of the assembled clergy's anger lies precisely in these canons, 2 and 3. The major target was not the common idolater—although he too was despised and excommunicated—but the flamen, the converted priest. Who was this flamen?

The flamen represented an old, established tradition of cultic life,

---

7. Tertullian *De Idol.* 1ff. and *De Spect.* 8. Origen *Exh. Mart.* 1ff. *Acta Sanctorum Scilitorum* 1ff.

created and sanctioned by the empire.[8] In charge of the imperial cult, he was the emperor's priest in the provincial towns, enjoying both cultic and secular functions as it behooved a representative of emperor worship, that shrewd mixture of religious ideology and political calculation. From the ranks of these municipal flamines was chosen the provincial flamen, the leader of the provincial assemblies, the *concilia*.[9] These flamines exerted a certain civic as well as religious leadership in the life of the provinces, acting at times as liaison with the imperial power structure itself. They did not come from senatorial blood, yet they rose, as inscriptions tell us, from only one stratum below, the equestrians;[10] therefore, they were part of the provincial elite. The priests of the imperial cult were vital figures in the provincial towns, especially in Spain, where, thanks to the famous inscription of Tarragona, emperor worship can be traced back to its very beginnings under Augustus.[11]

Some of these flamines had converted to the Christian church (2, 3) or were about to convert (4), and with that group the council of Elvira clashed in its opening session.[12] All flamines addressed in cans. 2–4 must have been converts. The empire would hardly have elevated practicing Christians, nor would a Christian have accepted this kind of pagan office. Flamines, then, were a special group. As converts they were tempted, under sanctions such as persecution or political pressure would produce, to either completely (2) or partially

8. On municipal flamines, see Jules Toutain, *Les cultes païens dans l'Empire Romain* (Rome, 1967), vol. 1, pp. 152ff.; H. Leclercq, "Flamines," *DACL* 5, col. 1643–51; A. Pauly and G. Wissowa, *Realencyklopädie der klassischen Altertumswissenschaft*, vol. 6 (Stuttgart, 1893ff.), col. 2490ff.; Stephan McKenna, *Paganism and Pagan Survival in Spain up to the Fall of the Visigothic Kingdom* (Washington, D.C., 1938), pp. 13ff.

9. Jürgen Deininger, *Die Provinziallandtage der römischen Kaiserzeit, von Augustus bis zum Ende des dritten Jahrhunderts* (Munich and Berlin, 1965), pp. 128ff.

10. *CIL* 2.4200. Deininger, pp. 102, 124, 152.

11. Quintilian *Inst. Orat.* VI. 3.77. Robert Etienne, *Le culte impérial dans la péninsule Ibérique d'Auguste à Dioclétien* (Paris, 1958), pp. 362ff.

12. The material in H. Leclercq, col. 1646ff., is misleading. Leclercq cites archeological evidence for the Christian flaminate, but all the evidence dates from a later period by which time the transformation of the office of the flaminate had taken place. No inscriptural evidence exists which would indicate that Christian flamines were common at the beginning of the fourth century.

(3) fall back to reaffirming their former pagan loyalty. A real issue at the opening of the synod must have been, therefore, the social conflict between clerics and the converted flamines in their own ranks. The decisions in cans. 2–4 make it absolutely clear that the church was not dealing with one or two exceptions, but that it was facing a number of municipal dignitaries of whom some were still catechumens (4) but others certainly had undergone baptism (2): "qui post fidem lavacri et regenerationis." When the council met, the bishops struck immediately at that group. Although a convert is eager to obey, he is also less reliable than those born into the faith. To control their former rivals, especially those equal to them in prestige and power, must have afforded eminent pleasure to the Christian clergy of Spain.

One must admit it is a significant development in the social history of imperial Rome that a flamen should have become a baptized Christian. He was an equestrian and held an office that had been important through three centuries of imperial religion. The conversions of flamines to the Christian church, for which the imperial propaganda had had nothing but pure contempt, are a remarkable demonstration of the loss of vitality in the office of the flaminate during the last decades of the third century. One cannot explain why members of such an aristocratic group should undergo catechumenate and baptism and join a despised group, unless they sensed that the church was on its way to power and that in its dynamism lay new social and political opportunities. The conversion of flamines to the Christian church presages the crumbling of the traditional anti-Christian momentum of the imperial socio-religious power structure years before Constantine defeated Maxentius at Milvian bridge.

Why did the synod assume the flamen to be such a threat? The severity of the council's sanctions against betrayal by converted priests was the last act of rivalry between the Christian bishops and the pagan flamines, that final triumphal assertion of power which victorious groups love to hurl in the moment of victory. The hostility against the flaminate in these opening canons can be explained only by assuming that a power struggle for the cultic leadership of city and province had gone on, perhaps for decades, between bishops and flamines in Spanish *civitates*.[13] After all, a duumvir, who also had to be present at idolatrous ceremonies, came off very easily (56).[14] The flamen, therefore, and not the duumvir, was the main rival. Hence, we can understand the vindictiveness of these clerics when some of their conquered foes fell back, and also the impulse behind the passionate can. 17 with its d^5 threat, prohibiting marriage with a pagan priest. This rivalry is an understandable concomitant of the analogous roles of the two leadership groups: both bishops and flamines symbolized a cultic ideology, both belonged to important provincial councils, and both performed vital sacrificial acts for their followers, the flamines presiding at state ceremonies, the bishops over eucharistic celebrations.[15] They were natural contenders. The bishops won. The archeological evidence on the flamines proves the demise of their power. In the last quarter of the third century the inscriptional evidence on the flaminate disappears.[16] This does not mean, of course, that the flamines disappeared. Elvira shows that they were very much alive. The office continued, with different functions, in the age of Constantine, but the vital public role of the flaminate was waning. Precisely in the decades just before Elvira the shift from flaminate to episcopacy must have entered its decisive stage. The first canons of Elvira show the last stage of that shift. Flamines had come over to the church, yet their conversion was not secure enough to prevent some of them from compromising with the empire under external pressures. It may be that the council's anger about the behavior of the

13. The existence of a *flamen Augustalis* in Baetica is confirmed by *CIL* 2.3271.

14. The duumvir's office was not merely administrative and political (*Lex Urson.* 94), but had religious connotations (*Lex Urson.* 128).

15. K. M. Setton, *Christian Attitude Toward the Emperor in the Fourth Century* (New York, 1941), p. 18.

16. Etienne, p. 502. There are 77 inscriptions of the imperial cult under the Antonines, 94 in the third century; however, eighty-five percent of those who can be identified as donors of inscriptions were city officials. The seeming absence of councils is due to the general sparsity of documents at the end of the third century (Paul Guiraud, *Les Assemblées provinciales dans l'Empire Romain* [Paris, 1887, reprinted Rome, 1956], p. 220).

flamines was one of the immediate causes for summoning the bishops to Elvira: the bishops of Baetica and of other provinces in the Iberian peninsula, taking no chances on having their victory over the flaminate jeopardized, called the council to make sure their control of the converted priests was maintained.[17] That settled, the bishops turned to the other grave issues relevant to the building of their own empire.

What was the nature of this clergy who dared to deal so arrogantly with some of the most illustrious converts the church thus far had made? An answer to this question lies in the canons themselves.

THE EMERGENCE OF A CLERICAL-IMPERIAL ELITE

The canons of Elvira reveal a Christian clergy that acted out a new kind of leadership in the municipal life of their provinces.[18] In case after case bishops made far-reaching decisions on the daily life of thousands of people in their towns. They distributed sovereign judgment, mercy, harshness, leniency. Analysis of the constantly alternating decision patterns reveals how capriciously the individual choices were made, but this did not matter. The bishops did presume to threaten their fold, and in this presumption lay their power. *Divide et impera*: some Christians were thrown out, some were kept in; some were promised final reconciliation, some could cleanse their sins with all kinds of penance. The early church was never sure where the boundary lines should be drawn between christian and unchristian behavior, and neither were these bishops and presbyters. But by enacting alternating decisions, by throwing out, for instance, certain flamines (2, 3b) while keeping a door open for others (3a, 4), they displayed their power to rule and their ability to offer the secur-

17. Cans. 1–4, belonging to the beginning of the corpus, represent the kind of mood that prevailed at the opening of the council. Notice the difference between cans. 1–4 and cans. 19 and 73–81.

18. Otto Seeck, *Geschichte des Untergangs der antiken Welt*, vol. 2 (Berlin, 1901), p. 181.

ity of a redemptive community for members of their flock in distress.[19]

I speak about a new elite, a clerical priest class acting as new municipal leaders of the province. The canons show an elite class that has actually several gradations. It divides at least into two, an episcopal elite and a clerical elite. The people who assembled and who made the decisions were presbyters and bishops. They saw themselves in a separate class, the *clerus* (80), and they acted as *clerici* (20, 27, 33), distinct from the *laici* (81). When these presbyters and bishops made their pronouncements they spoke for the trifold clerical group of bishops, presbyters, and deacons (19, 75); at times, they spoke for members of the lower clergy as well (33). Within the trifold higher clergy the council clearly saw the deacons in the lowest rank (77). The very fact that the synod emphasized bishops and presbyters indicates these clerici played the major role in the church.[20] In other words, there was a group which identified and functioned as a clerical group. In addition, however, there is clear evidence of another identity, that of an episcopal class consciousness within the clerical group. A series of canons reckons with the bishops as the major authority in the church (28, 38, 53). Can. 27, demanding of a cleric that he live only with a sister or a virgin, addresses itself to bishops and only secondarily to other clerics. Can. 58 treats the bishop as a key figure in the church. All five canons suggest an episcopal class consciousness in the clerical group at Elvira. The two identifications belong together. There is a clerical identity in which the individual felt himself apart from the lay flock of the church, and there is an episcopal identity in which the bishop felt himself above the presbyters and deacons who had been trained to look up to him.[21] Who, then, made the decisions of Elvira? Are these clerical or episcopal decisions? The

19. The control over attendance at church (cans. 21, 46), over public behavior: *eo quod minime sit cognita vita* (can. 24), over Christians who claim to be confessors: *litterae communicatoriae* instead of *litterae confessoriae* (can. 25), over persons asking for promotion (cans. 24, 53).

20. The lessening of the deacons' power was continued at Arles, can. 16.

21. Dale (p. 84) speaks rightly about "episcopal supremacy as the fundamental conception of the new order."

major figures were surely the bishops, but the presbyters voted with them and identified with them. It is probably impossible in retrospect to separate these two identifications, not only because we do not possess minutes of the sessions that would show the distribution of the weight of influence wielded by the individual men present, but also because the two identifications may have been intermingled very closely.

Patristic models of authority were always hierarchic, never democratic. The church followed the political trend toward greater autocratic power, a process greatly speeded up since the age of Aurelian and Diocletian.[22] The bishops became more and more powerful as time went on until the strongest of them set themselves up as primates of the churches at Rome and Constantinople. The synod of Elvira struggled ineffectually with this development toward major ecclesiastical sees without actually committing itself (58), although similar moves toward centralization were going on in North Africa, Egypt, and elsewhere during the fourth century. The synod of Elvira gives a good example of multiple patristic models of hierarchic authority: clerical-collegiate, episcopal-collegiate, episcopal-autocratic, patriarchal.

These clerics of Elvira had become a new urban elite.[23] They would not have dared to play with the equestrian priests of their towns unless they had felt equal to them. As cans. 2–4 demonstrate, equal they were, the proud members of an aggressive new cultic elite. The clerics who travelled to Elvira were no longer sectarian leaders representing a minority religion comprised of poor and middle-class citizens and slaves of the empire. This synod contained in its midst, if not some *curiales*—as I would strongly suggest—at least citizens

22. The canons of Elvira belong to the political trend as well as to the legal one in which, since the age of Diocletian, Roman law became totally hierarchical (M. Rostovtzeff, *Social and Economic History of the Roman Empire* [1926], pp. 449ff.). Kaser, *Römische Rechtsgeschichte,* pp. 206ff.

23. Urbanization in the economic politics of Constantine (Clemence Dupont, *La réglementation économique dans la Constitution de Constantin* [Lille, 1963], pp. 197ff.). To be sure, Antonine emperors had already favored urbanization (E. S. Bouchier, *The Roman System of Provincial Administration* [Oxford, 1914], pp. 219ff.).

approaching such significant social rank.[24] A Christian who took on the important position of a duumvir in a Spanish town must have had important friends in the synod; otherwise, his exclusion from communion would have been longer than one year (56).[25] A simple Christian who did not have such connections was punished by a ten-year sentence merely for being present at the capitol when sacrifices took place (59)![26] One remembers in this context that only a very few years later one of Constantine's first acts was to free Christian bishops from the *munera,* a statute that reckoned with the presence of curiales among the clergy.[27] One can not find out, of course, who among the nineteen bishops present at Elvira could have been a curialis. But we do know that Ossius of Cordoba, who was present at the council and symbolized more than anyone else the new Christian leadership in the age of Constantine, came from a wealthy family.[28] He realized the dream of public power as no one among his brethren at the synod might have imagined it possible, becoming Constantine's religious adviser, and being sent out by the emperor to the provinces in difficult cases, thus serving as liaison between emperor and the provinces, as formerly the flamen had done. In a way, Ossius was Constantine's imperial priest, except that he took on a much more incisive task than a flamen had ever dared to take on, and with farther-reaching results. In his life journey from Elvira to Nicaea and Sardica, Ossius is a fascinating example of the bishop who dared to subdue, by sovereign canonic decisions, the noble converts of Spain.

24. A curialis was a possessor (can. 49), Ganghoffer, *L'évolution des institutions,* pp. 114ff., and Joseph Vogt, *Der Niedergang Roms* (Zürich, 1965), p. 484.

25. Only a few years later the synod of Arles treated magistrates even more leniently (cans. 7, 8).

26. According to the bronze fragments containing the municipal charters of Salpensa in Spain, the duumvir had to take an oath to Jupiter, to the deified emperors Augustus, Claudius, Vespasian, Titus, and Domitian, and to the municipal tutelary gods. *CIL* 2. 1963.

27. Eusebius *Hist. Eccl.* X. 7. 1ff.

28. Ossius, who was influential in creating the idea of an ecumenical council (G. Langgärtner, "Das Aufkommen des ökumenischen Konzilsgedankens. Ossius von Cordoba als Ratgeber Constantins," *Münch. Theol. Zeitschr.* [1964, 11ff.]) was, as Athanasius reports (*De Fuga* 5) a member of a wealthy Spanish family.

The bishops and presbyters had not acted merely on the basis of wishful thinking; they had read the signs of the times correctly.

The emergence of this new clerical priest class corresponds in time with the lowering of the ranks in the civil leadership of the Roman provinces. Ever since the third century, senatorial governors had begun to be replaced by equestrian governors. In Baetica, for instance, not much later than the time of this council, an equestrian is documented as *praeses* of the province.[29] As the equestrian class was taking on the governorships of some provinces, the new class of bishops moved up to capture the leadership of religious municipal life. The crisis of both the equestrian and senatorial classes in the third century helped the bishops in their social climb.[30]

The canons suggest that the council began to take on the role of a provincial assembly. For centuries provincial councils of the imperial cult, in the East called κοινά, in the West called *conventus, collegia,* or most commonly of all, *concilia,* had met under the leadership of an ἀρχιερεῦς or in Latin terminology, a flamen. Seventy years ago Lübcke proposed that the Christian synods of the second century originated in these provincial councils of the imperial cult,[31] a theory which was challenged by Harnack on the grounds of inconclusive evidence.[32] The problem of the origins of the Christian councils—a problem which, by the way, has not yet been solved—does not concern us here. By the time of Elvira, councils had been a long-established institution in the Christian church. The question to be raised, however, is whether or not such Christian councils took their image,

29. Hans Petersen, "Senatorial and Equestrian Governors in the Third Century A.D.," *Journal of Roman Studies* 45 (1955):54–55.

30. Rostovtzeff, p. 435.

31. K. Lübcke, *Reichseinheit und kirchliche Hierarchie des Orients bis zum Ausgang des 4. Jahrhunderts* (Münster, 1901), pp. 32ff.

32. Adolf von Harnack, *Geschichte der altchristlichen Literatur* (Berlin, 1893), pp. 797–98. E. Schwartz, "Ueber die Bischofslisten der Synodalen von Chalcedon, Nicaea und Konstantinopel," *Abhandlungen der Bayrischen Akademie der Wissenschaften,* N.F. 13 (1937), p. 39.

at least in part, from the concilia of the imperial cult.[33] I believe that the evidence speaks in favor of such an influence. The opening canons represent the last throes of a bitter struggle between flamen and bishop. But the flamen was connected inextricably with the provincial council, for those converted flamines with whom the bishops were fighting had of course presided, according to the requirements of their offices, at imperial concilia.[34] To connect the Christian council with the pagan assemblies whose former leaders were now in the Christian community is surely not farfetched; a group often accepts in part the image of the rival group it fights hardest against. Just as the bishops in part took on the image of the flamines, their rivals, the provincial representatives of imperial religion, so the Christian council in part was playing the role of its rival, the provincial assembly.[35] Indeed the Christian council, with its bishops, was soon to become a vital provincial force under the new Christian emperor and the new symbol, Christus Pantocrator.

To be sure, other conciliar assemblies existed, which fact contributed to the shaping of the synod's self-image. The municipal senates, for instance, meeting in the curiae near the *fora* of the towns, presented another prototype, the legislative body. The Christian council, in a way, paralleled both municipal senate and provincial concilium.[36]

33. The provincial council combined religious with administrative functions (C. H. V. Sutherland, *The Romans in Spain* [London, 1939], pp. 154ff.; E. F. Abbott and A. C. Johnson, *Municipal Administration in the Roman Empire* [Princeton, 1926], pp. 162ff.; H. Gelzer, "Die Konzilien als Reichsparlamente," *Kleine Schriften* [Leipzig, 1907], pp. 142ff.).

34. Etienne, pp. 172ff., 197ff., 217, 249. On the urban and municipal character of the pagan concilia, see Jean Gagé, *Les classes sociales dans L'Empire Romain* (Paris, 1964), pp. 173ff.

35. The rivalry arose partly from the crisis of the city bourgeoisie in the empire (Rostovtzeff, pp. 444ff.).

36. *Dig.* XLVII.14.1; *CIL* 2.4127; Hamilton Hess, 30ff. Other kinds of councils can be documented in Roman Spain: Suetonius *Caes.* 7.10, Livy *Hist.* 21.12 (see Giraud, pp. 219ff., 61ff.). How the bishops identified with the senators can be seen in can. 19; bishops were prohibited to do business, just as senators were prohibited to increase their fortune by commerce (Dio Cassius 69.16; *Cod. Theod.* XIII.1.21). My analysis of can. 19 has shown that the prohibition was, in fact, a weak one, and could not be enforced.

Furthermore, the Christian council exerted a much more aggressive control over the behavior of its subordinates than the council of flamines ever had tried to achieve or ever could have achieved. The bishops not only controlled the behavior of their congregations in ceremonial and liturgical affairs, but they made inordinate demands on the daily lives of the believers. They interfered in matters of marriage, they prohibited the admission of certain professional groups like charioteers and pantomimes into the church, and they forbade playing dice and even sought to control the economic affairs of their communities. With this interference the church transcended the merely cultic and representative demands of imperial worship and so won its spectacular social success.[37]

The canons reveal the ambivalence in the very image which the clergy had of themselves. They saw themselves at the same time as leaders of a persecuted minority movement and as the lawgivers for a new religion establishing itself in the empire. This dual image shows up strikingly in the two decisions of cans. 59 and 60. In the first, a Christian was not allowed, under threat of a stiff penalty, to walk to the capitol at a time of pagan sacrifices; in the second, churches were not permitted to accept as martyr anyone who had broken a pagan idol. The two canons, although both comprehensible in their intentions, are on opposite sides in the evolution of the church from an anti-imperial sect to a new imperial religion. While in 59 the church still voted as the greatest religious antiestablishment movement Rome had known since the Bacchanalia trial and the various revolts in the century and a half thereafter,[38] in 60 it voted as a new establishment that protected itself from certain rebellious forces in its midst.[39] Can. 59 pronounced a rigid d^4 ten year sentence which was

37. Christian political and social success parallels and feeds on the imperial development toward a "corporate state" (F. W. Walbank, *The Decline of the Roman Empire in the West* [London, 1946], p. 47).

38. Rigobert Günther, "Der politisch-ideologische Kampf in der römischen Religion in den letzen zwei Jahrhunderten v. u. Z.," *Klio* 42 (1964):246ff. As for the early empire, see Ramsay MacMullen, *Enemies of the Roman Order* (Cambridge, 1966).

39. Dale, p. 279. Also, compare can. 1 with can. 25.

angry and which could be successfully applied against the accused; 60 merely pronounced a vague d^2 decision which threatened no one, certainly no bishop or presbyter, and which primarily served as an expression of general agreement for the synod. Either there was no opposition at all to 60, or if there was, it apparently had no chance of being translated into an amendment. Perhaps two groups of bishops pressed for the passing of these two cases: those who advocated a continuing fight with Roman civilization proposed can. 59, and those who saw themselves as the coming new elite brought up can. 60. The fact that both of the canons passed without amendment proves that the synod's majority stood behind both of these decisions. The church that voted on both 59 and 60 felt itself at the same time a fighting sect and the emerging establishment.

The counterpull can be seen in the remarkably lenient way representatives of the imperial power structure were treated in cans. 55 and 56. The first of these punishes a priest *(sacerdos)*[40] who had not sacrificed in any form, but who had worn a crown, with two years' penance. The text does not call him a flamen, but this is what he probably was; if not, he belonged to a related group of priests. The second censured a duumvir by suspending him for the span of the one year in which he exercised his office. Flamen and duumvir came from the same social level and could be one and the same person, as inscriptions show.[41] Yet while in cans. 2-4 the flamen was treated as the archenemy of faith, in cans. 55 and 56 flamen and duumvir received the mildest sentences meted out by the synod: a d^4 two-year exclusion for what was indeed a mild transgression by a sacerdos, and a d^4 one-year exclusion for the duumvir. The synod exhibited, therefore, in these latter decisions a rather pro-imperial mood. This change of attitude indicates the presence of a profound tentativeness in the Christian leadership's feelings toward the established powers:

40. The difference between flamen and sacerdos has not been established definitively. Deininger sees no basic distinction (pp. 136, 149); Etienne sees geographic variations (pp. 190ff.). In Baetica, the municipal priest is sometimes called flamen, at other times sacerdos (Toutain vol. 1, p. 153).

41. *CIL* 2.3711. Dale, pp. 232ff.

they fought them bitterly, but they also felt an affinity to their position. While in the opening canons the bishops were willfully determined to subdue their rivals, in 55 and 56 they let an ambiguity stand which was present not only in relation to the imperial establishment, but to various groups within the church as well.

Cans. 73 and 75 reveal the degree of clerical self-protection which the council exerted. Can. 73a pronounced a d^5 sentence against a Christian for denouncing another Christian who thereby lost his life or property. This punishment, that seems reasonable enough, is reduced in the second sentence of the canon (73b): in case the denounced person does not suffer death or exile, the punishment was merely a d^4 sentence of five years. In a third decision (73c), the same d^4 five-year sentence is pronounced if the denunciation was engineered by a catechumen. If examined closely, these three sentences astonish even one who has gotten used to the fluctuating mood of Elvira. They say, in fact, that if a catechumen denounced someone and this person was killed, he received only five years' penance. If a baptized Christian denounced someone, and that person was tortured or jailed, instead of killed or exiled, the punishment likewise was only five years. Yet at the same council, a Christian received ten years merely for being present at the capitol during sacrifices. And a duumvir, who obviously had to be present during such a ceremony, received a mild one-year sentence of exclusion coextensive with the term of his duty.

The most crucial necessity for the members of this council, thus, was not to weigh the culpability of the denouncer against the culpability of the idolater, but to safeguard their own rank. Can. 75 makes this clear, punishing with a d^5 clause Christians who pronounce false witness against bishops, presbyters, and deacons. This canon, however, does not excuse catechumens, as 73 did, nor does it permit laymen any alleviating circumstances. The reason is unmistakable: the clergy was protecting itself in can. 75, while it protected the Christian general public in 73. Can. 73 does not say, of course, that clerics could not have suffered severely by such denunciation. Yet, a comparison between 73 and 75 reveals that when it came to protecting the clerical rank exclusively, the synod showed no mercy to the denouncer. It is this protection of the elite which accounts for the extreme d^5 decisions of cans. 2, 3, 17, 73, and 75.

The canons give us instructive information about the social and economic state of the people whom the clergy addressed and about their own economic position in the church of which they felt themselves the dominant leaders. The bishops and presbyters frequently tried to discipline people of means, and they acted as if they themselves were people of means holding important social positions in their towns and provinces. Can. 41a, for instance, prohibits Christian landholders[42] from having idols on their estates; in 41b the injunction is modified to allow the keeping of such idols if the Christian masters fear a violent rebellion of serfs or slaves in the event of the removal of such idols; in 41c the canon threatens these Christian landholders again in the case of their personally disobeying the church's ruling against idols. These landholders belong to the curial class.[43] In the ruling of can. 41 the bishops were not only attempting to force Christian discipline on the curial masters of estates, but they were also identifying with them by providing a mitigation that was a tacit acceptance of their social advantages. Can. 40 likewise addresses Christians in a privileged economic position, prohibiting them from accepting as rent anything which previously had been offered as sacrifices on a pagan altar. The canons presuppose that the master of the estate belonged to the church, but that the tenant did not. Can. 49 prohibits Christian landholders from having their crops blessed by Jews. In this ruling again the synod reckoned with the Christian estates of rural Spain and attempted to sever the ties between these

---

42. I translate possessores as landholders rather than landowners because large parts of provincial land belonged to the empire, and possession of land was not always identical with ownership. Fritz Schultz, *Classical Roman Law* (Oxford, 1951), pp. 428ff.

43. Gagé, pp. 379, 402.

estates and rival communities. All three canons meant to control the life style of a group of Christian curiales, while at the same time affirming their privilege.

Other evidences point up how frequently this synod addressed itself to the vested interests of the important or wealthy people of the provinces. Can. 57 prohibits the lending of gowns, a custom practiced by high officials.[44] Can. 67 does not permit women to have anything to do with hairdressers, a custom that again could apply only to people enjoying some luxury. In 24, 25, and 38, the synod reckoned with the fact that believers commonly travelled, and the latter two of these canons imply business activities. Conversely, can. 5 makes it clear that the clergy did not identify with the poor people of Spain. The flogging to death of an *ancilla* one would expect to have outraged the assembly. However, the mistress was actually treated quite leniently. In the eyes of these bishops the homicide of a slave was less of a crime than a walk to the capitol in time of sacrifices or a severe case of sexual misconduct. Long before the council of Elvira, a more humane treatment of slaves had been advocated by pagans than that practiced by these bishops.[45] Can. 5 indicates that the council had an astonishing callousness about the lives of human beings who happened to be of a low social order.

The council's domineering yet cautious approach to the members of the leading social classes within the church is expressed in the decision patterns of some of the canons just mentioned. Several of these (41, 49, 67) contain a d^3 sentence. Such levies sound unrelenting at first sight, but the fact that they include neither a command of penance (d^4) nor of ultimate exclusion (d^5) suggests strongly that they were negotiable. The clerics attacked certain customs of some of their richer flock without either meaning or daring to follow their sentences through. Can. 41 is especially instructive in this respect since it contains in its three separate parts the synod's attempt to control

---

44. Dale, p. 274.
45. *Scriptores Historiae Augustae Hadr.* 18.7: Gaius *Inst.* 1.53.

the curiales as well as the restraint growing out of the fear of going too far. The first decision is an exceedingly cautious d^2: If possible *(in quantum)* Christians should not permit idols on their estates. The second takes the prohibition right back: If they fear the power of the serfs, they may leave the idols where they are.[46] The third decision blasts the landholders again: If they don't abide by the ruling of the church they shall be kept out. However, even the third decision is only a d^3, not giving any span of penance, let alone anathema. A whole range of frustration and anger vis-à-vis these important members of their fold appears in weak d^2 and d^3 sentences. It was neither easy nor feasible to manipulate successfully these *possessores* who had too much economic power on their side.

At the same time, the attending churchmen themselves belonged to an economically privileged group and did not live a life of apostolic poverty.[47] The canon on usury (20) is in line with other antique legislation which frequently tried to stem the brutal practice of coercing huge sums of interest from desperate debtors.[48] The very fact that this canon had to be included in decisions of the synod proves that money or goods were at times lent at high interest by Christian clerics as well as laymen. The economic activity of the provincial leadership can be demonstrated in can. 19, which prohibits economic activities by bishops, presbyters, and deacons: They shall not do business in the provinces; if they need to make money, someone shall do it for them; if they want to do business, they shall do it in their own provinces. The canon, however, achieved very little, with its vague d^2 prohibitions which finally permitted the bishops to do in their provinces as they pleased. The last sentence actually takes back part of the force of the first and thereby reveals the tension in the council during the formulation of this canon. Without doubt, the conclusion can

---

46. Idols stood everywhere in Roman houses (Tertullian *Apol.* 13, *De Spect.* 8, *De Idol.* 15).

47. Athanasius *De Fuga* 5.

48. *Papyrus Berol.* I.210.105–6. See also Nicaea, can. 17 and Arles, can. 13.

be drawn that some of these clerics were involved in mercantile operations.[49] Whoever brought up this matter had the important men and the majority of the council against him since he did not even win a d^3 sentence, let alone a stronger one. It is possible that can. 19, and in its wake can. 20, were brought up by members of a conservative minority of bishops who clung to early patristic ideals, according to which monetary activity was incompatible with apostolic leadership. In spite of them, however, the council was not willing to reverse the trend by really effective curbs, for in the d^2 decision of can. 19 it accepted tacitly the degree of change in the economic status of the bishops who had stood up against the flamines in the opening canons of the synod.

Can. 19, then, accepts the economic changes attendant on the establishment of a Christian clerical elite. These economic developments become even more significant as one understands them in the context of the province of Baetica, where the council assembled. In the time of Strabo and Pliny, the provinces of Spain had been exceedingly prosperous,[50] but since the age of the Severian emperors, the Iberian peninsula had gone downhill with the rest of the empire. Municipal vitality had decreased as the towns were taxed out of prosperity, and in A.D. 261 the Goths had broken in and sacked Tarragona. Dating of potsherds of Monte Testaccio, typifying the rich export trade from Spain to Rome, indicates, for example, the end of the lucrative wine imports after the middle of the third century.[51] However, in the economic decline, the province of Baetica, the most Romanized of Spanish lands, was less affected than others by the

49. The problem had been with the church for a long time (Tertullian *De Idol.* 2, Cyprian *De Laps.* 6). The synod of Bacara II (can. 2–7) tried to eradicate the economic aspects of baptism, against which can. 48 of Elvira speaks. Dale, pp. 301ff.

50. Pliny *Hist. Nat.* 37. 203; Strabo, *Georg.* III.2.3–4. R. Thouvenot, *Essai sur la province Romaine de Bétique* (Paris, 1940), pp. 155ff. J. J. Van Nostrand, "Roman Spain," in F. Tenney, *An Economic Survey of Ancient Rome,* vol. 3 (Baltimore, 1937), pp. 119ff.

51. Ernest Nash, *Pictorial Dictionary of Ancient Rome,* vol. 2 (New York, 1961), p. 411.

general decay and continued to prosper, although in a limited way.[52] Not only was the city of Elvira located in Baetica, but the majority of clerics attending this council came from that province, which had been able to sustain a certain economic vitality. These bishops, as can. 19 shows, had been able to take advantage of the relatively viable economy of their province. The evolving episcopal-clerical elite of Spain was strengthened by the economic power displayed by the clergy of Baetica. These bishops and presbyters travelled, they played key civic roles in the towns, they knew important magistrates, they were able to lend money, and they disciplined rich people. It is no wonder that can. 19 was phrased so innocuously. To decide that a cleric should get involved in business matters only in his own province was but pure advantage to the majority of members from Baetica. It supported their own drive and it kept rivals out. It is also no wonder that can. 19 has neither d^3 nor d^4 nor d^5 in its sententia. The majority of members in that synod never meant to give up these mercantile advantages that could only enhance their new municipal role.

One more canon supports the clerical status described here. Can. 80 prohibits a freedman from becoming a cleric as long as his pagan sponsor is still alive. The purpose of this canon was to keep the clergy legally and economically independent of any pagan bonds. There was only a d^2 sentence, without any amendments and without further condemnations. Can. 80, of course, does not address itself to a majority of the clerics present. These bishops were certainly not freedmen. Spain had, as all the other provinces, many colleges of *seviri augustales* to which freedmen belonged.[53] However, the conflict behind the canons of Elvira was not with these *collegia* of freedmen, but with flamines and with the curial classes. Why, then, is there only a d^2 decision in can. 80? There are two possible explanations: either the synod did have a few important *liberti* in its midst and did not intend

---

52. Orosius 7.2; Eutropius 9.8. Van Nostrand, p. 219. Bouchier, pp. 39ff. A. Caldo, *I Severi, La crisi dell' impero nell' III secolo* (Rome, 1949).

53. Thouvenot, p. 272. Gagé, p. 367.

to touch them, or the synod did not think that the matter was very important—after all it was brought up at the very end of the debates—since the Spaniards present felt socially above close dealing with freedmen. In either case, the freedman problem was played down by the council, and understandably. These bishops did not intend to play the role of seviri but of equestrian priests.

COMMUNIO

The members of the church felt themselves part of a community, a redemptive community that was arcane-ritualistic and aggressive-public at the same time. The arcane character of their church was emphasized constantly: the synod operated with the baptismal symbol, marking the separation of the church from the world (1, 2, 37, 48), and with initiatory stages (gentiles/Jews/heretics—catechumens/ Christians/faithful),[54] categories which were designed to enhance the uniqueness and the privileged status of the faithful. The synod brought out the special character, the arcane value, of the community by grading punishments: the more securely a person was in the fold the more harshly he was punished for transgression. The synod also governed the community's liturgical customs: fasting (23, 26), Pentecost (43), the washing of feet (48). The public character, as I have shown, was represented in the fearless fashion the synod dealt with duumviri, flamines, and sacerdotes, and in the natural way it accepted the public and economic activities of its clergy.

The difference between the assured rhythm of the canons and the tensions in the various decision patterns shows that the leaders were not of one mind about which specific course that community should take. The clergy of Elvira were involved in the process of defining and redefining the character of the Christian community. The bishops of Spain did not come to the plains of Granada with a clearly developed blueprint of their communities' new roles. Their decisions would

54. The word *christianus* in 39, 45, and 59 refers probably to the person admitted to the catechumenate; such a use of christianus seems to be borne out, although from a considerably later date, by Council of Constantinople I, can. 7.

not have been so complex, so vacillating, and so equivocal, if they had known precisely where they wanted to go. They found out as they acted, as they formulated decision after decision. The canonic model, the phrase, the pattern, the sentence—these were the means by which the synod controlled and redeemed, the action through which their direction evolved. Although their ecclesia was three centuries old and proud of its past, it was itching to play its role in the province in more and more visible ways.

The need to redefine the community was due not merely to the change in the relationship between church and empire, but to the sheer increase in numbers of adherents. A sect as a minority group has an entirely different place in society than when it becomes numerically a major force. The Christian population of Spain by the time of Elvira had become considerable, as Arnobius tells us.[55] This increase demanded a reorientation of the liturgical and social practices, and it brought along a profound alteration in the self-consciousness and the functioning of the Christian elite. It was one thing to act as bishop of a small sect in Smyrna and it was another to represent a widespread cult with thousands of initiates in Baetica. Among other things, it was much more difficult for the leadership to dominate and to check on the lives of their people once the community was comprised of large numbers. Above all, it was no longer possible to operate with the world as the foe, when, for all practical purposes, the church itself in its popularity and influence had become the world.

Communio for the clerics of Elvira was, on one level, eucharistic: *communionem accipere* (1, 2, 8) meant to receive the eucharistic elements; *communionem dare* (13) meant to give the eucharistic elements to the faithful. The d^5 threat, prohibiting communion in the end, was a concrete refusal by the clergy to let a person be given the final eucharistic ritual by the church. Communio was certainly not only eucharistic, but defined the Christian community as a social as well as a cultic organism. *Sociari dominicae communioni* meant to

55. Arnobius *Adv. Nation.* 1.16.

share the Sunday communion of the church, to receive the elements of the eucharist, to participate in the exclusive community of the baptized. That Sunday communion itself, which the faithful had to attend strictly lest they be punished (21, 46), was one aspect of the Christian community as a social institution. It was the focus for the whole community that was affirming its public place, proud to be able to deal with flamines and duumviri. It would be entirely misleading to see in the d^5 sentences merely a sacramental measure.[56] Just as in Cyprian's letters, communio was alternatively both eucharistic and social, so in the arcane-public double role of Elvira's clergy, communio stood for the church's celebration and for its political power.[57]

How much communio was social as well as eucharistic can be measured from the synod's conflict with heretics and Jews. To belong to the Christian community meant not to be a heretic, to be distinct from the Jew. The Christian anti-Semitism prevalent to our day, and the medieval bigotry against the heretic helped define the communio of Spanish Christianity. The Jew was the scapegoat on whom the church could always turn. Economic factors may have operated, judging from Constantine's decision to forcibly return Christian girls who married Jews to the weaving factories from which they had been taken.[58] The Jew was above all, however, the enemy against whom the church could draw the boundaries which it needed so desperately: a Christian did not marry a Jew (16), and he did not feast with him

56. De Clercq, p. 109. Cf. also F. Dölger, "Der Ausschluss der Besessenen von Oblation und Kommunion nach der Synode von Elvira," *Antike und Christentum* 4 (1934):111–12.

57. Cyprian's communio is ecclesiastical (*Ep.* 15.4; 19.2; 31.8) as well as eucharistic (*Ep.* 16.3; 17.2). Tertullian *Apol.* 39.3–4: ". . . if any man has so sinned as to be banished from all share in our prayer, our assembly and all holy intercourse." Also, Tertullian *Apol.* 44.3, *De Paen.* 7 and 9; Cyprian *Ep.* 55.6: "because the church was shut against them." O. Chartier, "L'excommunication ecclésiastique d'après les écrits de Tertullien," *Antonianum* 10 (1935):341–42 and H. Grotz, *Die Entwicklung des Busstufenwesens in der vornizänischen Kirche* (Freiburg, 1955), p. 350.

58. From the Constantinian age on, the Jew was the social, political, and religious enemy. *Cod. Theod.* XVI. 8.1; Eusebius *V.C.* 3. 17ff.; Ambrose *Ep.* 40; Laodicaea, cans. 29, 37–38; Toledo III, can. 14; *Apost. Const.* 69. James Parkes, *The Conflict of the Church with the Synagogue* (New York, 1961), pp. 151ff. and Solomon Katz, *The Jews in the Visigothic and Frankish Kingdoms of Spain and Gaul* (Cambridge, 1937), pp. 3ff.

(49) or accept religious blessing from him (50). To have sexual relations with a Jewish woman was especially bad (78). In all this ancient Christian hatred of the Jews, economic, psychological, social, and liturgical matters were intermingled. The Christian communio had to distinguish itself, to set itself apart.

The heretic was the second scapegoat. He too threatened the security of the communio because he too was related closely to the church. Hence, there are the s^3 units of can. 16, giving metaphysical-biblical undergirding to the desired separation between faith and heresy. The canons of Elvira make it quite clear that heresy was a social phenomenon (16, 22, 51): the often-taught distinction between schism as social and heresy as theological is misleading.[59] Even when the council takes exception to a divergent liturgical custom as heresy (43), it attacks a social separation, since liturgical plurality disrupted the unity of the church. Just as *peccatum* was an antisocial act (22), so *credere* was a communal act (62). A *fidelis* was a member of a community (9). By using the heretic and the Jew as targets the community built up its exclusivity.

Did the bishops of Elvira have any theological concerns at all? The absence of christological and trinitarian formulas, so shortly before Antioch and Nicaea, could mislead one into believing that the Spanish church was totally uninvolved in the ideological and speculative enterprise of Christianity. Such an assumption would be absolutely wrong. Ossius of Cordoba, present at the council, was deeply involved in the christological problematic. Gregory of Elvira, writing two generations later, had certainly an intense interest in theological questions. Also, the Priscillian turmoil showed that in Spain as elsewhere speculative theological problems could lead easily to controversy and schism. Compare the canons of Elvira with those of Nicaea. If we were in possession of the decisions of the latter council only, we would not realize how fanatically that council was involved in specu-

59. Heresy represents not merely a belief with which the church disagrees, but a label pinned to a rival group. One transfers from a heresy: *transitum fecerit* (22); it is a *societas* (16), a group one comes from (51).

lative problems. The canons of Elvira demonstrate the kind of social reality into which the ideological beliefs of ancient Christianity were translated and in which they functioned. There existed a baptismal theology, as we see from the reference to those "who, after the faith of saving baptism" (1). There existed an exclusive saving ecclesia which the fathers of the church expressed by *mater ecclesia,* ark, body of Christ. As a matter of fact, the canons of Elvira express both sides of the patristic problem of whether the church was a pure virgin, consisting of the saved and, therefore, excluding the sinner, or was a nourishing mother, an ark comprising both the pure and the less pure. There also existed the image of a new man, a redeemed man.[60] The patristic axiom that God became man to make man divine was translated into social and psychological terms: to be a man of salvation was not to play dice (79), not to fornicate (30), not to share in sacrificial ceremonies (59), not to lend gowns (57), not to disobey or certainly not to betray the clerical hierarchy (73, 75). To be sure, this Spanish translation of theology into social reality looks quite primitive to the modern observer, but does the translation practiced by the synods of Ancyra, Nicaea, Sardica, or Toledo look any more sophisticated and "theological"? The decisions of all these councils were not phrased by an Origen, a Justin Martyr, or an Augustine, but by the average patristic leadership, intellectually not especially astute, by that grass roots elite which brought the Christian communio to its victory.

Who, then, was a Christian?—one who belonged to that communio. Yet, since there were so many Christians, and since it had become so difficult to separate christian behavior from that of others in the social context in which the church was intermingled every day, on what points should a Christian draw the line? If one wants to have a redeeming community one must say from what that community is redeemed. It is that necessary though artificial drawing of the borders which Elvira's clerics tried to achieve in their canons.

60. The old man is cast off: *veterem hominem dereliquisse videatur* (can. 46). The videatur is very significant for the ambiguity I have pointed out.

They singled out certain civil office holders: not senators, not *aediles*, not *questores*, not *decuriones*, but flamines and duumviri. They were tough to the flamines, with a major emphasis on d^5, and lenient to the duumviri, with only a one-year d^4 exclusion. They singled out those in certain occupations which had become social targets for the church long before: pantomimes, charioteers (62), prostitutes (44, 12). They could have chosen others, those also rejected by the Christian tradition, like soldiers, artists, or gladiators, but they did not.[61] They singled out very few targets among the many social customs of the pagan culture: not the funeral feasts, not the garb of clerics, not the many magical practices, from the evil eye to the magic of love, practices with which the church in succeeding centuries had to cope with great pain.[62] Instead they chose playing dice (79), lending gowns (57), throwing coins into baptismal fonts (48), having hairdressers around (67). Some customs, like the use of torches at funerals, were rejected by an angry d^3 sentence, although the custom was only partially rejected in that candles only at daytime were forbidden. To be a Christian, therefore, meant not to burn candles (34), not to spend vigils (35), not to have pictures in churches (36). In these cases the synod chose safe issues and targets. One pantomime entertainer or charioteer more or less did not make much difference to the church, so these could easily be dismissed *(d³)*. The duumvir was another matter, which is why he got off so lightly, with only a d^4 one-year sentence. Libelli famosi had been prohibited in the pagan world ever since Augustus, so the synod did not have to muster much courage to hit people practicing that custom (62).[63] Again, the d^3 sentence did not

61. Tertullian *De Spect.* 15–16; 22–23; Arles, cans. 4, 5. *Apost. Trad.* rejects actors (12), charioteers (14), and gladiators (15). It is strange that the synod did not struggle with the problem of soldiers. Even if Baetica did not, the other Iberian provinces did have a vast military network. The synod apparently saw no conflict.

62. On the threat of witchcraft and sorcery, see *Cod. Theod.* IX. 16.3. Can. 6 does not challenge *maleficium* proper, but only homicide by maleficium. Magic was widespread in the ancient world (Tertullian *Apol.* 43.1; Ancyra, can. 24), and so was the use of torches (Virgil, *Aen.* 11. 142ff; Tacitus *Ann.* 3.4). Can. 34 does not represent the early Christian stance against the use of torches (Minucius Felix *Oct.* 38; Tertullian *De Idol.* 15), but a transitional attitude, leading to the acceptance of the custom in the age of Constantine (Eusebius *V.C.* 4.66).

63. Dio Cassius 56.27. In the age of Constantine, the Edict of Lyttos 5.

CHAPTER THREE

counter a major threat. To play dice was·no great crime so a d^4 one-year sentence was sufficient. In Elvira's patterns of decisions against customs and against Christians involved in pagan civic life, many of the decisions were insignificant. The basic issues, represented by the d^5 sentences, were actually few. Yet, the synod really fought on those issues: idolatry, apostasy, protection of its own hierarchy, homicide, and above all the matter of sexual control, to which I turn in the next chapter.

At the council of Elvira, a group of Spanish bishops heralded the arrival of a new social order in which the Christian carrier of power was to play a vital role. They set the tone of ecclesiastical decision-making of the future, having found in the canon a powerful model of control. The synod led to other synods; the model of Elvira was copied, developed, augmented. To be sure, the bishops did not gain all they perhaps had hoped for. They did not receive actual imperial administrative power,[64] and had to share their new elite status with two other groups, the new administrative and military elite classes. Only much later, when the Christian ruler became a territorial prince, was the dream of Christian clerical power actualized, though for a short time and in a limited way. As the history of fourth-century Christianity shows, the rise of the Christian bishops to imperial status did not bring about great peace in the world but led to bitter conflicts between the church and secular authority and among the bishops themselves. But the turn had come, and the Spanish canons of 309 are among the best documents on which to base an analysis of the dynamics of that turn. The date of 309 suits best that very moment of transition, suggested by my analysis of the canons,[65] the

64. Ganghoffer, p. 196.
65. I take the year 309, suggested long ago by Mansi and again by H. Grégoire ("Les persécutions dans l'Empire Romain," *Mém. Acad. Roy. Sc. Lettres, Beaux Arts de Bélgique* vol. 2 [Bruxelles, 1951], p. 78) as the most probable date for the council of Elvira. De Clercq (pp. 87ff.) has defended at length a date prior to the Diocletian persecution by posing the problem of dating in terms of choosing between two great scholars, Hugo Koch, who argued from certain canons for the year 306 ("Die Zeit des Konzils von Elvira" *Z.N.W.* 17 [1916]:61ff.) and L. Duchesne ("Le concile d'Elvire et les flamines chrétiens," *Mélanges Rénier* [Paris, 1887], pp. 159ff.), who argued

period of a decisive ideological and socio-political change in the course of which Sol Invictus and Augustus Imperator were replaced by Christus Victor and Christus Imperator, and Vesta, Venus, and Isis were replaced by Mary.

---

from other canons for a date prior to that persecution. My analysis of the canons leads to a different approach and supports a date after the persecution, preferably 309. The canons are ambiguous; they are pro-Roman but they are also anti-Roman. There are canons that definitely suggest a Spanish church in peace but there are other canons which definitely point toward a preceding persecution. The ambiguity results from the ambiguous character of Spanish Christianity in its relation to the imperial power structure. Baetica was highly Romanized (Rafael Altamira, *A History of Spain* [New York, 1949], pp. 48ff.); the bishops at Elvira represented the cities of Baetica and of the major Romanized cities at the East coast. It is not astonishing, therefore, to find relatively little polemic against the Roman establishment in their statements: the bishops were about to take an elite place in the provinces themselves. Many scholars operate with the fundamental misconception of large-scale persecutions in the Latin world. The Diocletian conflict between church and empire in Spain was not what it was in Cappadocia, Egypt, or Palestine. There does not exist any verifiable evidence for a Spanish bishop's martyrdom during the Diocletian persecution. None certainly appears in Prudentius' *Peristephanon*. It is quite possible that there were severe actions against Christians in the North and in the West; but such actions were not taken against the bishops who assembled at Elvira. Ossius of Cordoba was not killed. Neither was any of the bishops at Elvira mutilated, as was the case with bishops at Nicaea. Therefore, the canons which indicate some conflict with Rome but no great persecution in the style of Galerius or Maximinus the Dacian can very well be placed after the date of 304 or 305. After all, as Eusebius himself tells us (*Mart. Pal.* 13.12), the persecution in Spain was over in two years. To assume the institution of a Christian flaminate for this period is unfounded. The archeological evidence about Christian flamines points to later periods when under the Christian imperium the office of the flamen was taken over into the Christian context. The flamines at Elvira were converts. It is this kind of upper-class convert who would be most in danger of lapsing under social and political pressures, such as a persecution ordered by the empire; it is also this kind of convert who lends himself, due to his uncertainty and fear, as a tool and test case for the elite group that rose to eminence in Spanish civitates. I plead for 309 rather than 306 because it seems to me three or four years between the end of the persecution and the beginning of the council explain the relatively mild attitude toward the church's struggle with Rome better than a span of one or two years. Man forgets fast, especially if the conflict he is about to forget did not touch him as deeply as he thought it did at the time. The date of 313 is certainly too late, not only because it would be difficult to explain the whereabouts of Ossius, but because the socio-political ambiguity in the canons is much better explained if they were written before Constantine enacted the great change in the fall of 312. The date of 309 fits the time of change, after a limited persecution, limited at least in the municipalities of Southern and Eastern Spain; it fits the turn of the great tide, from the Diocletian to the Constantinian relationship between Christianity and secular power; it belongs to that transitional period in which the issue of idolatry was about to be replaced by the issue of asceticism as the focus of Christian identity.

Four

THE SEXUAL DILEMMA

In the turmoil of a decaying empire the Christian church attempted to find its communal identity; in the crisis that had come about at the twilight of antiquity, the Christian elite sought to carve out a clerical image. Both of these struggles rose to the surface whenever the synod of Elvira dealt with matters related to sexuality. By establishing sexual codes the synod meant to define the particular character of Christian life; by setting sexual taboos the synod meant to limn the image of an ascetic clerical leadership. No matter how ambiguous these ideals turn out to be on close analysis, they were of far-reaching import for the history of Christianity. Few ancient texts provide such evidences and opportunity to examine the purpose behind the Christian elite's antisexual drive as do these canons.

Sexuality represented a major problem to the participants of this council. No other issue, be it the unity of the church, the administrative hierarchy, the relationship to pagan customs or the conflict with imperial worship, was as prominent. The synod spelled out minutely, for instance, one case after another against adultery: adultery committed frequently (47)—d^6, d^5; once (69)—d^4; a second time (7)—d^5; with Jews or pagans (78)—d^4; by bishops, presbyters, and deacons (8)—d^5; by a cleric's wife (65)—d^5; by a layman's wife (70)—d^5, d^4. The synod passed sentences against all kinds of sexual misconduct: divorce (8), fornication (30), prostitution (12), homosexuality (71), abortion (69). The only accepted sexual expression was in marriage,[1]

1. Preferably one marriage, without a second marriage; can. 38 does not allow a *bigamus*, a person who is married a second time, to baptize a catechumen in emergency.

and that only within the Christian fold and only within the ranks of the laity, although the synod had to reckon with the fact that a large number of Spanish clerics were married. The inclusive term for sexual misconduct, moechia, designated the entire scope of transgressions from the officiating of flamines at public functions, ceremonies, plays, which might be regarded by Christians as obscene or sexually objectionable (2, 3), to the lovemaking of young people (14, 31) and adultery (65, 70).[2]

Two tables in chapter 3, above, express the extent of sexual legislation at Elvira. The first one (table 3), enumerating all of Elvira's d^5 decisions, demonstrates that the majority were directed against people breaking the sexual taboos of the church. These levies comprehend a much larger number of canons than the remainder of the d^5 decisions together, including those imposed for the serious matter of idolatry. In the second (table 4), which shows the range of topics taken up by the council, cases explicitly related to sexual control appear thirty-seven times, considerably more frequently than any other single issue with which the synod dealt. More than forty-six percent of the canons in the body of decisions deal with sexual transgressions, and the gravest available anathemata are applied against them. Taken together these two facts mean that control of sexual behavior was beginning to play a pivotal role in the church. Presumably the bishops and presbyters came to Elvira in order to deal with the apostasized flamines and the problem of idolatry, but the tables make it clear that as the synod went on in its deliberations, its prime concern was not apostasy, but sex.

We may well wonder what was going on in that church that almost half of the synod's legislation dealt with sexual matters.[3] What

2. Moechia, by the time of Elvira, had become an inclusive word used for sexual deviation and any grave social misconduct related, even only remotely, to sexuality (can. 2–3; Augustine *Conf.* 2.6).

3. I have limited the canons dealing with sexuality to the most obvious cases: marriage, prostitution, adultery, separation, pre- and extra-marital intercourse, abortion, homosexuality. The canons against pantomimes (62), hairdressers (67), and women spending nights at tombs (67; cf. the pagan *bustuariae*) have sexual undertones. So does the canon dealing with the sadistic killing of a slave woman (5).

were the purpose, the role, the extent of the sexual restraints the church sought to impose in the dynamic of the conciliar event of A.D. 309? I discern two basic functions of such legislation: the establishment of social coherence in the church's search for identity, and the creation of a clerical image which was to strengthen the clerical hold on the faithful.

SEXUAL CONTROL AND THE ESTABLISHMENT OF CHRISTIAN IDENTITY

Who was a Christian and who was not? In the age of the persecutions this question could, at least theoretically, be answered clearly: the Christian was a member of a church that fought under the banner of its own historical claim, Jesus of Nazareth, and its own mythological force, Christ as Kyrios. It fought against the religious status quo, represented by the empire with its ideology. Once this conflict began to disappear, however, serious identity problems arose. How could a church assert its uniqueness once it became imperial, once it played the political role of its former enemy? The canons are efforts at such assertion. A first function of the sexual legislation at Elvira was to help the Christian church enhance its inner cohesion at a moment when less and less cohesion could be gained from a vanishing conflict with its traditional imperial foes. By controlling the sexual behavior of its people, the clergy asserted its power. Cans. 15, 16, 17, and 78, taken together, demonstrate how the synod, by employing sexual taboos, tried to prevent any ties of the Christian church with rival groups, Jewish, heretical, or pagan (see table 5).

According to this survey, the misconduct of adultery did not differ substantially from the misconduct of contracting a marriage with a member of an outside group. To allow one's daughter to marry a pagan priest ($17—d^5$) was a much greater offense than to commit adultery with a member of an outside group ($78—d^2, d^4$). To commit adultery with Jews or pagans was sometimes less offensive than to permit one's daughter to marry a heretic or Jew ($16—d^4$). The penalty against a Christian who reported his own sexual misconduct was more lenient (78—d^2) than the penalty against a Christian who allowed his daughter to marry a Jew (16—d^4). Yet, this synod certainly went on the assumption that free sexual expression was a major evil and that the only acceptable form of sexual activity was in marriage. The basic axiom would have been: marriage is acceptable, adultery is horrible. Yet, when it came to marriage with outsiders, adultery suddenly was not worse than marriage. The contra-

TABLE 5

DECISIONS ON PROSCRIBED SEXUAL TIES

Transgression	Condemnation Pattern	Canon
Marriage with a pagan	d^2	15
Marriage with a Jew	d^4	16
Marriage with a heretic	d^4	
Marriage with a priest	d^5	17
Adultery with a pagan:		78
confessed freely	d^3	
denounced	d^4	
Adultery with a Jew:		78
confessed freely	d^3	
denounced	d^4	

NOTE: All the d^4 decisions in this table represent a five-year exclusion.

diction is significant. The major purpose of the sexual decisions at Elvira was not to preserve the institution of marriage, per se, except as it operated restrictively upon sexual activity. Basic to the council was the intention to keep the faithful within the Christian fold. The concern to control the community was much more important than the purity of the individual.[4] Marriage and adultery had one thing in common: they established intimate ties with members from rival communities and thereby threatened the church's unity. Through

4. *Cod. Theod.* XVI.8.6 is an excellent example of how in imperial Christianity economic, social, and religious factors worked together in producing legislation on sexual control: women in weaving factories, who had been married by Jews, were forced to return to their factories. See also *Cod. Theod.* III.7.2, IX.7.5. Roman legislation had prohibited intermarriage between Romans and Egyptians *Pap. Berol.* I.210.52.

its sexual legislation, the synod safeguarded the Christian community against encroachments by its rivals.

However, the legislation also furthered an image of what it meant to be a Christian. By defining, in canon after canon, the acts which a Christian does not commit, the synod exposed, from the negative of the photograph, so to speak, a picture of an authentic believer. He was a person who lived, sexually, a precisely circumscribed life: no premarital, no extramarital, no heretical, no perverted love of any kind, not even in youth, not in widowhood. By this ideal of purity or exclusivity, the synod described Christian identity. It drew a line, artificial, but highly effective, between acceptable and nonacceptable sexual behavior and called the latter "crimen" (18), or "scelus" (35, 63), saying to the Christian in effect: If you keep within the line we draw, you know where you belong. There were other groups outside the line, like pantomimists, charioteers, and dice players, who did not belong in the Christian fold. In the early Christian era a man who betrayed the church by pagan sacrifices had not belonged inside. But the fact that 45.7% of the canons of Elvira ruled on sexual matters indicates a shift in emphasis. Sexual behavior had become the prime medium through which the Spanish church sought control and definition.

However, the church's attempt to define a Christian as a person who lived a life of sexual exclusivity ran up against two major obstacles. In the first place, the very fact that dozens of canons had to deal with believers breaking the code which was meant to give them identity proves how far the image was from the reality of practice. In the second place, the heretics and Jews against whom the church tried to hold up its image of purity were certainly not morally inferior to the Christians. The Christian church, as the antiheretical literature shows in chapter after chapter, always tried to discredit its rivals as sexually inferior, an apologetic slander technique that has worked to this day. But, in fact, the Jewish tradition valued images of sexual purity no less than did the Christian church, and many of the heretical or schismatic churches split off precisely because they displayed an ethos superior to that of Catholicism.[5] Furthermore, the empire itself had taken violent measures to fight the widespread practices of divorce and adultery.[6] The categorizing of extremely limited sexuality as part of an ideal about man certainly was as present in the rival movements as in the Christian church.

The tension produced by the discrepancy between fact and wish can be examined in the s^3 unit of can. 16, which is indicative of the way the church defended itself against its rivals. The text prohibits intermarriage with Jews and heretics "since there can be no community for the faithful with the unfaithful." The unbelievers of this scriptural quotation (2 Cor. 6:14) were not pagans, but Jews and heretics, two groups who, by their histories and by precisely their beliefs, were related closely to the Christian church.[7] The unbelievers were comprised of the Christian's own kin, they represented their past, and at times presaged their future. After all, in the eyes of many bishops in Eastern provinces of the church, the orthodox of Spain might have appeared as heretics. The purpose of the s^3 unit, based on the Pauline antithesis, was to polarize two related traditions in order to widen the chasm between the church and its rivals by slandering the latter as unbelievers—a phenomenon that occurs time and again in the history of religion. With its s^3 unit the church tried to frighten the subservient believer from stepping across the blurred and fragile boundary lines between the church and those groups closest to it.

While a first purpose of the sexual canons of Elvira consisted in strengthening the social coherence of the church by implying an ideal of Christian laic life, a second purpose lay in establishing clerical identity.

5. Novatian, Donatist, and Meletian splits occurred precisely because the schismatic group opted for stricter discipline than the major provincial Christian establishment.

6. Regarding the fanatic attempt to stem widespread adultery through legislation by the Antonine emperors and their followers, see *Cod. Just.* IX.9.2ff. and the similarly fanatic laws of Diocletian (*Cod. Just.* IX.9.19ff.).

7. The original primitive Christian use of the word *unbeliever* can be seen in Tertullian *Ad Uxorem* 1.2; Cyprian *De Laps.* 6.

THE CREATION OF CLERICAL IDENTITY

By applying different value scales to certain individuals and groups within the church, the synod promoted in its sexual legislation the vertical separation, long present in the church, between "higher," more rigorously governed believers and the average laity. There are, for instance, two canons about virgins: the first (13) condemns a special kind of virgin, girls who have taken the vow of chastity *(quae se Deo dedicaverunt),* while the second (14) deals with the unmarried girls in the Christian communities. Both types of virgins are condemned for having made love to a man. They are punished, however, by two widely unequal levies: while the higher virgin is thrown out for good, the average girl in the church is desciplined by one- or five-years' penance, depending in each case on whether or not she married the man. In can. 13a the penalty is d^5, while in 13b it is d^6. In can. 14, however, the penalty is the less severe d^4: a one-year exclusion in 14a and five years in 14b. Measuring the same transgression by such vastly different standards, the church leaders enforced a distinction between special and average believers. They hit the special virgins very hard and seemed to give them, thereby, a privileged position in the life of the communities.[8] However, in so doing, they actually enhanced their own image as sexually pure representatives of the Christian elite.

The canons single out the clergy from the laity. They exacted a pattern of behavior from their members distinct from that expected of average believers. While for the same sexual misconduct, girls from the laity were more or less lightly punished (14) and dedicated girls received at least a slight chance of mercy (13), the clergy had to take anathema without mercy. While a layman was given a d^4 five-year sentence, a cleric received a d^5 sentence for the same deed. A

---

8. The church had had difficulties with its "virgins" all along, 1 Cor. 7:36; Irenaeus *Adv. Haer.* I.6.3; Tertullian *De Virg.* 17. The virgins were kept in tightly controlled dependence by a promise of greater reward, Pseudo–Cyprian *De Habitu Virg.* 23; they were promised better habitations in the heavenly mansions.

sexual transgression during adolescence, in can. 31 punished vaguely
(d^2), led to a subdeacon's deposition (d^3) in can. 30.

This distinction is extremely important in the history of the Catholic priesthood because it helped to form the clerical leadership image. In the famous can. 33 of Elvira, the church for the first time demanded *expressis verbis,* in a canonical decision, sexual continence of its married clergy. In a somewhat awkward formulation all clerics were asked to abstain completely *(in totum)* from their wives, and not to beget children. This canon, contrary to frequent interpretations, does not talk about celibacy. Its goal is not, or at best is only indirectly, to enforce celibacy. The canon directed its force against the married clergy of Spain by insisting on a marital relationship without sexuality; it does not command celibacy, it prohibits the sexual act.[9]

Can. 27, conversely, was directed at the unmarried clergy. It prohibits them from living with anybody except a sister or a daughter, and not just any daughter, but only one who had dedicated herself to the religious life *(deo dedicatum)*. It is in connection with such cases as these that the methodology devised here is most fruitful. The two decisions were phrased in two different patterns. Can. 27 against unmarried clergy arrives at a d^2 sentence, but can. 33 against married clergy declares the harsher d^3. The distinction is extraordinary. The d^2 decision of the first is vague: the canon does not threaten those who disobey with deposition or with any other penalty. What happens if some bishop's sister comes to live with him? The canon does not come to terms with any such question. The d^3 decision of the second is determined: There shall be no intercourse, no children, or you shall be defrocked. The synod clearly hurled a much stronger warning at the married clergy than at the celibate.

It is impossible, of course, to determine the exact circumstances which produced such differentiation. On a large scale, it expresses the

9. That can. 33 prohibits intercourse involving married clergy and the begetting of children by clerical couples is of great importance to historians of clerical celibacy because it demonstrates the extent of sexual fear involved in the development of the clergy.

evolution toward a celibate priesthood, where the married priest was by definition always in the wrong. That process, however, had begun long before Elvira and was not completed until many centuries later. Some concrete struggles must have gone on in that synod which· account for the two different decisions. It may be that the synod expected greater resistance from the married clerics and hence was more categorical, even angry, in its d^3 decision. It is possible that the synod did not intend to enforce 27, while it did mean to carry out its threats in 33. It is also quite possible that this differentiation reflects a power struggle between younger, unmarried, aggressive clerics and an older group. One detects in 33, for example in the in totum, an element of envy, perhaps frustration on the part of the person, or persons, phrasing the sententia, resenting the opportunity of sexual gratification for others which was denied to them. Whatever factions were in the synod no longer can be determined. The difference, however, between the two decisions supports what we know from other evidences in the rise of clerical power, that the church was not of one mind as to what it meant to live a life of clerical-sexual exclusiveness.

On one matter the clerics agreed: their asceticism marked their separation from the average believer. The man who makes such sacrifices, the cleric who lives so much more "purely" than the layman, feels he has the right to demand the privileges of leadership. This image of clerical purity helped the ancient Christian clergy to establish itself as a special and superior group in the church, one leading a more perfect life. While the old priest elite of Spain, the flamines, had to be married, the new priest elite, the Christian bishops, presented a counterimage, responding to the need of the time: an ideal of man renouncing, even when married, the sexual "temptation."[10] In the proximity of sexual decisions and leadership decisions the canons of Elvira reveal perhaps better than any other patristic text the close connection in the ancient church between the clerical

10. Sexual purity and priestly power belong together (Tertullian *Exh. Cast.* 7).

taboos against sexuality and the formation of a clerical elite.[11]

The clerical ideal of sexuality was far from firmly established, however. There were two groups addressed by the council: celibates (27) and married priests (30, 33, 65, 81). As cans. 18, 30, and 65 show, the concrete experiences in the church showed quite a different reality from that which the ascetic image envisioned. To be sure, the image served the clergy well, since—as we will see later—the laity asked for it and the clergy felt strengthened by it. Nevertheless, in these sexual canons designed to control the church, there is a great deal of frustration and ambiguity, due to the tensions in the lives of the formulators between the clerical image which they propagated and their daily lives in which they exerted their leadership. A case in point is the attitude of the council toward women that is revealed in the canons.

THE CLERICS AND WOMEN

The clerics of Spain forced themselves to live a life without sexual intercourse. Yet, those same clerics dealt with women all the time in the business of the church. The resulting repressed sexuality caused by the prohibition against any normal sexual outlet led to the clerics' constant desire to punish the women with whom they came in contact: women (8, 9), catechumens (11), virgins (13, 14), widows (72). The synod censured women for all kinds of daily habits: going to a cemetery (35), lending clothes (57), having hairdressers around (67), writing letters (81). Taking for granted the double standard prevalent in the Roman culture,[12] the Christian clergy meant to control the women in the churches. More than one-fourth of the canons are directed expressly against women:

11. The phenomenon was widespread, of course. What the canons of Elvira demonstrate is the emergence of the combination of cultic-sexual purity and Christian socio-political control.

12. In the *Lex Julia*, wives had no right to bring criminal charges against their husbands in cases of adultery, while the men were granted that privilege, of course (*Cod. Just*. IX.9.1). Cf. the mild treatment of men in Arles, can. 10.

d^1: There is one positive decision in regard to a woman: a "redeemed" prostitute is to be accepted immediately into the church (44).

d^2: In three cases a straightforward prohibition without further qualification was pronounced: against the woman who leaves an adulterous husband and marries another (9), against women frequenting cemeteries (35), and against women who write letters (81).

d^3: An angry stricture was passed against women having hairdressers around.

d^4: There are three ten-year sentences: against a woman who lives with another man, but who leaves him (64), against a woman who commits adultery with the knowledge of her husband, but who thereafter leaves him (70), against a widow who cohabits (72). There are three five-year sanctions: against a catechumen (11), a girl (14), and a widow (72); and there is one sanction of one-year's exclusion against a young girl who made love to her bridegroom before marriage (14).

d^5: An astonishingly large number of nec in finem sentences were passed out against women: those who leave their husbands (8), dedicated virgins who transgress (13), women committing abortion, both .baptized and unbaptized (68), women living with another man until their death (64), unfaithful wives of clerics (65).

d^6: The reversal of ultimate punishment was decided on five times: twice in the case of catechumens (10, 11), once in the case of a dedicated virgin (13), of a woman who remarried (9), and of a widow (72).

The survey shows how much the synod tracked down in great detail the sexual transgressions of women, and applied all kinds of punishments. The large number of canons directed against women is certainly considerably higher than it was in nonecclesiastical documents of the time. The decision patterns employed against these Spanish women reveal a male aggressiveness, if not hostility, on the part of these clerics: six radical anathemata and three d^4 ten-year sentences reveal a need on the part of these clerics to single out women as objects of punishment. In a way the clerics teased the very persons with whom they interdicted any overt sexual relation.[13]

A comparison of these decisions reveals blatant contradictions. A girl who had made love before marriage was punished by one- or five-years' exclusion (14); a prostitute was received into the church without any reservations (44). It paid to have been a prostitute rather than a virgin girl in view of such ecclesiastical sanctions.[14] While the bishops let the *meretrix* enter the church instantly, they removed a subdeacon who had had sexual intercourse, even though the act had occurred long before his term of office (30), in his youth perhaps. The contradictoriness is striking in the case of the mistress who killed her slave girl (5). I have not included that canon in the list of sexual decisions, although sexual undertones were present in the synod's describing, then passing judgment on, the sadistic act of a Christian woman against another woman. The bishops treated the woman who had brutally beaten a girl to death considerably more leniently than, say, a woman who committed abortion (63, 68): it was obviously less threatening to the synod to talk about an act that only implied a sexual sadism that might have been unconscious on the part of the participants, than about acts which were overtly related to lovemaking. When the synod punished the mistress of can. 5 so lightly, it did not comprehend or confront the repressed sexuality in the woman's homicidal act, let alone its own arbitrariness in handling the case.[15]

The ambiguity toward women appears also in can. 72. In an oscillating emotional wave, the canon goes through four different responses, disciplining widows in the church. A d^4 sentence of five years is prescribed in 72a, a d^5 decision in 72b, a d^4 decision of ten years in

13. Sexual sadism can be seen everywhere in imperial marriage legislation of the third and fourth centuries (*Cod. Just.* IX.9.30). Otto Kiefer, *Kulturgeschichte Roms* (Berlin, 1933), pp. 66ff.

14. *Apostolic Tradition* 16.20 branded prostitution.

15. *Ex.* 21:20–21, more than a thousand years earlier, let the master go free if the slave survived a day or two. Elvira ignored the humanitarian tendencies of the second century. Constantine continued Elvira's sadistic trend (*Cod. Theod.* IX.12.1–2).

72c, and a d^6 decision in 72d, for having sexual relations with a man; it gives her the full anathema for having sexual relations, but marrying yet another man. In a third decision this strictness is reversed in favor of a ten-year penalty, and, finally, the canon pronounces a chance of mercy. In one canon the synod expresses three different emotions toward the widow: a desire to discipline her, a rage to hurt her without mercy, and a certain clemency.[16]

The aggressiveness, hostility, and ambiguity in these decisions, the clerics' need to punish and tease the women of their churches, are fully comprehensible as a natural result of the sexual restrictions which they imposed on themselves. The clerics denounced the sexuality which they had to deny themselves—or which had already been denied them by their ascetic predecessors in Spanish church life—and for which they yet longed. While the monk could flee into the desert where even a sublimated relationship to a woman was reduced to pure fantasy,[17] the bishop was caught up day after day in the tension between his natural attraction to the opposite sex and the social repudiation of sexuality to which he was committed. The frustration rings in the formulation of the d^3 decision of can. 33. The canon sets up two demands for the clergy: to abstain from their wives and not to beget children. In the first command of the canon the second was obviously included. The man who designed the sententia vented his frustration by adding the second phrase. How could anybody in Spain find out if the command to abstain from their wives was totally kept? So the man proposed the second prohibition, not to beget children, which could be verified. The real crux, however, was not the prohibition against children, but against the sexual act.

Did the synod, in setting up sexual taboos in canon after canon, both in respect to clergy and to the laity, deal realistically with the

---

16. Can. 72 can be read two ways. Either all four decisions are directed against the widow, or 72c and 72d are directed against the man whom the widow marries. Despite the fact that the latter understanding prevails in traditional studies (Hefele, p. 259), I opt for the former because the construction of the canon is really much clearer, the subject of *non accipiet* being the widow, *qua vidua*.

17. Athanasius *Vita Ant.*

problems of sexual freedom? What exactly was the relationship between the ideal of sexual purity proposed by the church and the
reality of daily life in that same church?

THE CLERIC AND HIS CHURCH

The sexual canons of Elvira were certainly not the mere fantasies of
a clerical peer group, but resulted from actual situations in everyday
life. Typical of the canons of Elvira is that they deal with concrete
cases; they are not judgments made in the abstract: a Jew blessed the
fields of Christians (49), servants demanded of their masters permis-
sion to keep idols on their estates (41), a Christian walked up to the
capitol (59), a heretic came over to the Catholic church (51). The
canons on sexual matters, likewise, clearly are based on actual situations: subdeacons were caught by rumors about their past (30), a
Christian slept with a Jewish woman (78), women lived with other
men (64), Christian girls married heretics (16). The disparity between the implicit intention behind the ascetic ideal formulated in
the canons and the social reality to which it applies is clear. Sexual
infractions, both in the ranks of the laity (14, 31, 63ff.) and of the
clergy (18, 30, 69), were obviously common. The very phraseology of
certain canons, furthermore, reflects the gap between ideal and reality.
In can. 78, for instance, the synod distinguished between believers
who reported their sins on their own and those who were denounced.
The purpose of this distinction was to coerce the covert sinner into
confessing his sin. In making such a distinction the synod in fact admitted its fear that sexual ideals were broken by larger numbers than
those already accused. In can. 9 the synod first prohibited a woman
who had left an adulterous husband from marrying someone else
(prohibeatur ne duceat); yet immediately after phrasing this first decision, the synod continued: "if she does marry" *(si duxerit).* The first
command, cast in the vague d^2 pattern, was obviously not intended
to be taken at full face value by the synod. As we have seen, these d^2
decisions are symptomatic for revealing precisely those injunctions
which the council either did not mean or did not dare to enforce by

a strong levy of penance or exclusion. What appears in the vague phraseology of the d^2 decision is the half-acknowledged feeling of frustration about the difference between the council's ideals and the limited chance of their changing the habits of the believers. In other words, their control over the sexual life of their provinces was at best tenuous. And they knew this.

They proved they knew it by creating a double standard under the terms of which the clergy was more rigorously punished than the laity for offenses, and by which, reluctantly, they allowed a certain sexuality to the laity. After all, the institution of marriage could not be obliterated altogether; otherwise Spanish Christianity would have died out. In this double standard, in the distinction between a perfect life and the life of the average married layman, the primary motivation was the social and psychological desire of the clergy to control the laity, and not a benevolent acknowledgment of their sexual needs. Whatever sexual rights the layman was allowed were granted as a means of controlling him. The layman was the oppressed.[18] That the sexual life of the church was regulated by the perspective of an ascetic elite group explains the frustration into which the frustrated clergy of the patristic church threw the Christian laity for centuries to come. Yet, one cannot hold the clergy alone responsible for patristic anti-sexual legislation. The clerical image worked; otherwise the clergy would not have been able to impose it. After all, the layman approved it. He found relief in being governed by priests who seemed to live a life of purity. It worked because it spoke to the layman's aspirations for clerical ideals, even though in the layman's own life these ideals were not honored.

SEXUAL DUALISM

When the church of Elvira guarded a celibate cleric so fully from the other sex that it hardly permitted him to have any woman in his resi-

18. 1 Cor. 7 was a compromise between Paul's ideals (7:1, 7:7–8, 7:29) and the needs of his addressees (7:2ff., 7:9, 7:36ff.).

dence even to perform the housekeeping chores, and when that same church tried to compel married men to live with their wives without sexual intercourse, it was involved in and trying to cope with a widespread crisis phenomenon, sexual dualism. By sexual dualism I do not mean merely the ancient duality and the conflict between sexuality and society which expressed itself in Hellenic and in many other traditions as the tension between mind and matter, but a tipping of the scale so against sexuality that sexuality becomes synonymous with evil.[19] The sexual act becomes abhorrent and people either flee into deserts or write books on the perfection of virginity. At such a stage we are no longer dealing with conflicts but with crisis.

What is this crisis to which the canons of Elvira, like so many other patristic texts, try to respond? To use a commonplace contemporary phrase, one could talk about an identity crisis, a serious confusion about sexual roles, what it means to be a man and to be a woman. Patristic writers, sometimes only vaguely and sometimes quite pointedly, connected the idea of a human fall with man's sexuality, attributing the painful or even tragic life predicament which man experiences to his tragic sexual relationship with women. When the young Augustine had an erection in the baths, his pagan father was proud, but his Christian mother was ashamed. Yet, long before he saw in concupiscence that act which recreated the first fall through all of history, Christian authors, at least implicitly, connected sexuality with evil.[20] The man was ashamed to be a man; his mother was ashamed to see him become a man. To be sure, patristic texts pose the problem almost exclusively from the male perspective, a fact which scholarship all too often fails to take into consideration. We do not really know much about the women of the church. Patristic texts, through which we find access to the hopes and fears of ancient man, were written,

19. Marriage and fornication differ only because the law says so, Tertullian *Ad Uxor*. 6; *Exh. Cast*. 9.
20. Augustine *Conf*. 2.2ff. There is a strong countercurrent in Gangra, cans. 1, 9–14; but, like the balanced position of Clement of Alexandria, it is exceptional.

with extremely few exceptions, by men, and of those, by clerics or believers strongly advocating the ascetic life.[21] What these texts and what the decisions of Elvira show is a crisis in male identity.[22] In the image of manhood which these canons presuppose, the woman as a sexual being was excluded. Where such sexual dualism was predicated, man no longer defined himself in relation to woman ("He created them male and female") or expressed the conflict creatively ("therefore a man leaves his father and his mother and cleaves to his wife"); instead he defined himself in separation from the woman. Origen, for example, followed the ascetic trend in the church and became a eunuch by his own hand![23] For the male priests at Elvira, the sexual act, prohibited in can. 33, would have jeopardized their role.

The flight from heterosexuality can be read everywhere in the century before and after the synod of Elvira. The vestal virgins received renewed attention in the third century.[24] A Persian-Gnostic sect, the Manicheans, advocating for its elect total repression of any sexual outlet, arrived in the empire only shortly before Elvira. The emperor Diocletian issued an incensed edict against the movement, but the empire had also promulgated violent legal curbs against adultery.[25] The empire's hysteria in both of these proclamations betrays how insecure the culture had become about the traditional Roman attitudes on matters of marriage and divorce. The writings of Cyprian and Tertullian, the pamphlet *De Habitu Virginum* by an unknown Christian at the end of the third century, Athanasius' books on virginity and on Saint Anthony, encouraged the faithful to admire a Christian

21. An exception is the *Martyrdom of Perpetua and Felicitas* which, at least in its main parts, reflects the psyche of a patristic woman, beautifully expressed, for instance, in Perpetua's dream about her dead baby brother (M. L. von Franz, "Die Passio Perpetuae," *Aion* (1951), pp. 116ff.).

22. *Evang. Thom.* 114: "Every woman who makes herself male will enter the Kingdom." *Exc. ex Theod.* 26.2–3.

23. Eusebius, *H. E.* VI.8.2; Matt. 19:12.

24. A. D. Nock, "A Vision of Mandulis Aion," *Harvard Theol. Review* 27 (1934): 53ff.

25. A. Adam, *Texte zum Manichäismus* (Berlin, 1954), pp. 82–83. *Cod. Just.* V.26.1; IX.9.9–10, 27, 30.

ideal which rejected sexuality in favor of innocence, purity, and virginity.[26] In Christian art the nude was to disappear.[27] All are evidences for the widespread uneasiness about man's sexual nature, and of the wish to deny basic human corporeality. Plotinus was "ashamed to be in a body."[28] His shame betrays the same fear which drove thousands of Egyptians into the desert where they could live free of all economic and social responsibility for women. A stream of movements, all trying to cope with man's experience of the demonic in life, theological and philosophical as well as artistic, inside and outside the Christian church, seemed to be responding to a general need for escape from sexual turmoil. Seventy years after the synod of Elvira, Gregory of Naziansus summarized his epoch's fears when he wrote about the "soul's unlovely loves for lovely bodies."[29] The Christian theologian was as much ashamed to be a bodily man as was the Neoplatonic philosopher a century before him.

The narcissistic reactions offered by these different movements to man's disturbance about his heterosexual nature have in common that they enabled him to find an escape from direct, concrete relationship to women, either by creating a metaphysical abstraction, by objectifying and spiritualizing sexual language, or by treating women as if they were asexual or in a presexual stage of life. The Gnostic movements, intent on formulating for man a speculative cosmogony as a means of finding out who he was, projected sexuality onto the cosmos; they answered ancient man's desperate search for his place and

26. Virginity is on an equal plane with the state of the angels, according to Novatian (De Bono Pud. 7). Tertullian accepted marriage even in his Montanist period (De Monog. 1), but he came to favor continence more and more (Exh. Cast. 10).

27. F. W. Vollbach, Early Christian Art (New York, 1961), plates 4, 5, 6, 40, 78, 118, 180, 218.

28. Porphyry Vit. Plot. 1. To be sure, Plotinus tried to say that the body was not bad in a primary sense (Enn. I.8.4); but he accepted it reluctantly and unwillingly (Enn. II.9.18). Real life was beyond the body (Enn. VI.9.8). The clearest philosophic expression of the negative attitude toward the body are in Numenius Chalc. in Tim. 298, Jamblichus Peri Diaph.; in C. J. Vogel, Greek Philosophy, vol. 3 (Leiden, 1959), p. 430.

29. Gregory of Naziansus Orat. 27.9.

origin in life by offering him sublimation in a cosmic construct filled with sexual imagery (bridal bed, sperm, begetting, *syzygia*);[30] they actually promised him in their aeonic dream world an epicene hope, an androgynous pleroma in which the definite characters of man as man and woman as woman were effaced.[31] What can be traced in these reactions is something like an individual's regression to infancy, a turning back to a stage of undeveloped or partially developed sexuality. Many patristic writers, for instance, present virginity as the ideal of human life, as if a preadolescent form of behavior was superior to that of the mature sexual person. The Spanish bishops, in can. 33, envisioned for their clergy a kind of marriage possible only if a sexual awakening, a sexual encounter, had not ever taken place. In can. 27 they treated their single bishops as if to have a member of the other sex in a cleric's house were a crime. Iconographic representations of baptism time and again depicted Jesus as a boy in the Jordan river, although according to New Testament texts he should have been shown as being of mature age. A large segment of the populace apparently demanded that a religion offer a presexual ideal of man.

The roots of the patristic crisis of sexuality can be traced back several centuries. In the Jewish tradition, for instance, people began to allegorize the *Song of Songs,* interpreting it as expressive of the bond between the soul and God. This act revealed the flight from, but also the persisting preoccupation with, sensual love. A Christian apostle advised his readers to stay single rather than to marry; the Jewish Christians who created and transmitted Matt. 5:28 saw in the very sexual desire a sign of adultery; Montanus taught his followers to

30. The question had been raised centuries before (E. R. Dodds, *The Greeks and the Irrational* [Berkeley, 1951], pp. 175ff.). In Gnosticism the projection of biological sexual phenomena into metaphysics (Robert P. Casey, *The Excerpta ex Theodoto of Clement of Alexandria* [London, 1934], p. 16) had led to extreme agony produced by the identity crisis of the Second Century A.D.

31. Material in my *Language of Faith* (New York, 1962), pp. 33–34. Instead of speaking about the "Mysterium der Geschlechtlichkeit," as Quispel does in *Gnosis als Weltreligion* (Zurich, 1961), p. 34, one should speak about the "Sublimierung der Geschlechtlichkeit."

break up their marriages; Origen committed self-castration; Tertullian wrote a pamphlet, *Ad Uxorem*, that is filled with indications of sexual fear; Methodius spiritualized the experience of love.[32] The phenomenon is not limited to any geographical or theologically exclusive sector of the church. Just as we find it outside Christianity in the theological and ascetic transcendentalism of Neoplatonism and in the dualistic speculations of Manichean cosmology, we find it within the church among heretics and Catholics alike, Greeks as well as Latins. Certain sects offered communal solutions to the dilemma, either in ecstatic antisexual movements such as Montanism or in the more or less disciplined monastic groups, some of which were perhaps influenced by Buddhist monastic ideas; while other sects offered an intellectual metaphysic, in the form of sublimated cosmic speculations, or a variety of ethical patterns and social images replacing or sublimating sexual concerns, such as virginity, the purity of the priesthood, a theology of the church as mater ecclesia and ideals of perfection.[33] When the bishops and presbyters arrived at Elvira to deliberate the state of the Christian union, they brought along the heritage of three centuries of confusion about the role of sexuality among Christians whose identity was already blurred in the worsening dilemma of the age. The uncertainty of the elders of the church was, of course, part of the growing uncertainty in the larger community. The clergy could therefore threaten their people by sexual canons because the faithful were in such crisis that they welcomed clerical control.[34] The inhabitants of the empire would not have sought access to the church in such great numbers, long before Constantine had established Christianity as the imperial religion, had that not been so.

I have not found a satisfactory theory which reveals fully the causes leading to the widespread sexual anxiety in the ancient world. The

32. A great deal of excellent material in E. R. Dodds, *Pagan and Christian in an Age of Anxiety* (Cambridge, 1965), pp. 8ff., 38ff.

33. Hugo Koch, *Virgo Eva-Virgo Maria* (Berlin, 1937); J. C. Plumpe, *Mater Ecclesia* (Washington, D.C., 1943).

34. The need of the laity can be read in the popular apocryphal novels of the ancient church: the *Acts of Peter*, of *Andrew*, of *Paul*, of *Thomas*.

very fact that similar phenomena came up in cultures totally unrelated to the Graeco-Roman cosmos indicates that such a crisis, given a certain set of circumstances, can arise easily. I offer a number of suggestions which explain in part the antisexuality behind the canons of Elvira.[35] A first cause responsible for the ancient identity crisis can be found in the tensions accompanying the creation of the *orbis Romana*. In a process extending over several centuries, the Romans achieved what the Hellenic age had begun to prepare long before: they gave Mediterranean man the first taste of a transprovincial consciousness. Paul of Tarsus felt like a proud citizen of the Mediterranean cosmos. The empire was his domain, he made his plans in terms of Greece, Asia Minor, Rome, and even Spain, and he travelled as a matter of course over provincial highways and Roman sea routes. Yet he felt definitely as a Jew, a Benjamite Jew, a Greek-speaking Jew. He was provincial and man of the empire at one and the same time. To enable such a double identity to exist marks the history-making achievement of the Roman dynamic; it meant a significant, if only a rudimentary and politically quite deficient, step toward the universal coexistence of discordant cultures.[36]

However, a costly price had to be paid for such an achievement. To sustain multiple identity demands of an individual considerable personal strength. An experience of pluralism and syncretism represents under the best circumstances a threat to one's security; if personal strength is sufficient, the pluralistic experience can be sustained and thereby become creative; if the threat proves to be too strong, a crisis sets in. The sexual dualism of the ancient world could be compared to precisely such a crisis: the tensions between an individual's own municipal or provincial culture and that of the imperial one, the

35. A great deal of work has to be done in patristic scholarship in order to understand the antique "failure of nerves," the crisis of ancient man (Dodds, *Age of Anxiety*, p. 1ff.).

36. Nobody can be a citizen of two countries, Cicero claimed (*Pro Balbo* 11.28); but such dual identity is precisely what Rome offered its provincial inhabitants (Lawrence Waddy, *Pax Romana and World Peace,* [London, 1914]).

tensions produced by the strata of dialects and languages, the tensions in having to identify simultaneously—to give one example—as Roman, North African, Numidian, and Berber, were simply overwhelming. A growing number of people asked in desperation: where do we belong? This agony expressed itself in sexual anxiety or escape from sexuality altogether. One can measure the extent of this socio-psychic phenomenon of "lostness" from the spectacular success of movements trying to cope with it: monasticism, Gnosticism, Manicheism, Neoplatonism, and Catholicism all offered an arcane social experience, an exclusive-esoteric community in which man found a place where he felt "in," sometimes through strict social rites, sometimes through a sophisticated meaning-canopy that made sense only to the initiate, sometimes through a discipline that separated the male from the rest of the world. The acute rise of what I call sexual dualistic language and the rise of arcane religions both fall in the centuries where the tension between provincial-tribal-municipal and imperial-Mediterranean identities began, between the second century B. C. and the second century A. D.

A second cause for the crisis lay in the extent and character of Roman urbanization. The empire produced city after city which was filthy, noisy, and overcrowded, cities where apartment blocks were face to face with slums, markets, baths, palaces, and temples, cities that were extraordinary melting pots where administrators and merchants from all over the world mingled with slaves, intellectuals, and soldiers, as well as with the native population. These urban centers became extremely vital for the evolution of a sense of individuality. Their multiplicity and syncretism created transprovincial and cosmopolitan attitudes that can hardly be overestimated in the light of history. At the same time, however, these cosmopolitan centers generated a disquieting uncertainty in the individual, who often lost his tribal and provincial ties in his experiencing of the brutality and loneliness as well as the heady spontaneity and excitement of an urban mass culture. The economic depression in the third century deepened the feeling of insecurity experienced by the masses and by intellectual leaders as well.[37]

In the urban crisis man feels the loss of his rural past. The mystery cults, existent in Spain as in the rest of the empire, offered archaic symbols which fed man's longing to "return" and provided him with a primitive blood bath, as in Magna Mater, or by the symbolic re-enactment of the primal killing of a bull, as in Mithraism, or by allowing him to share in the orgiastic feast of grapes, as in the cult of Dionysus.[38] Many of these cults permitted sexual practices that went against traditional sexual practices and customs. The priests of Cybele, for instance, castrated themselves, the girls who underwent initiation into the exclusive circle of brides in the Villa dei Misteri at Pompei were nude, the initiates of Mithra shared in exclusive male ceremonies that included torture and masking.[39] While urbanization brought forth, on the positive side, a widening of man's perspective and a keen emergence of his individuality, on the negative side it helped to create the kind of crisis which we find in the canons of Elvira. All the elements of that crisis and the reactions of arcane cults to it were present at the council, for the bishops were urban leaders; they controlled a community that by its extremely strong arcane discipline, through ritual and ideology, separated itself from the contextual culture and thereby offered man a place of security; they offered all this exclusive cultic life in images of strong nonsexual ideals.[40]

37. Rostovtzeff, pp. 416ff.

38. P. Paris, "Restes du culte de Mithra en Espagne," *Rev. Archéol.* 4.24 (1914): 1ff. Ramòn Pidal, *Historia de España* (Madrid, 1935), pp. 434ff.

39. Thomas Freedam, "Some Notes on a Forgotten Religion," *Psychoanalytic Review* 41 (1954):9ff.

40. Many patristic scholars are reluctant to operate with social and psychological categories. A great deal of research is done as if Freud, Erikson, Norman O. Brown had never written. E. R. Dodds (*The Greeks and the Irrational*) felt compelled to apologize in several places for his presentation for fear of being attacked. However, observers of the patristic church in the past have without qualms employed the categories of their centuries, the thirteenth, sixteenth, or 19th century, and demonstrated thereby that they shared in the hermeneutic evolution of history. The contemporary reluctance shows the extent of the conflict between theology and behavioral science.

A third factor operating in sexual dualism has to do with the religious crisis of antiquity, the death of myth. The process began long before the Romans established their hegemony over Carthage and still goes on today, but a crucial stage in that process can be located in the centuries preceding and following the birth of the Christian era.[41] In his mythological tales, man had created a framework by which he could justify himself and through which he could explain his dilemma. Myth ceased to function when it began to be understood, and this comprehension appeared, albeit for only a very limited segment of people, in both the Hebraic and Greek cultures. Amos slandered the Baal of Bethel; Hosea laughed about men kissing calves; Euripides saw Zeus as a force of nature; Xenophanes observed that if we were oxen our gods would look like oxen; the Greeks used allegory to explain away the offensive anthropomorphism of Homer, and Philo did the same in regard to the embarrassments in the Book of Genesis. These heretical reactions arose from man's expanding consciousness both of himself and the world and from the critical capacity of the human mind. They paralleled the development of universalism and urbanization, and they were not unrelated to man's technological and scientific experiences, in which man learned to predict, for instance, the eclipse of the moon, and to the experience of syncretism, in which man learned the relative quality of religious statements. At the same time, these insights undermined the various mythological frameworks which had been effective for thousands of years. At first for only a small segment of artists and intellectuals, then gradually for merchants as well as for slaves, the old religious security began to give way. One can read the extent of this mythological collapse by taking

---

Yet I do not believe we can talk meaningfully about the problems of fear, anxiety, identity, about urbanization, individualism, isolation, and projection, when we neglect the categories of the fields that struggle in the most concentrated and contemporary ways with precisely such problems.

41. Material in E. R. Dodds' *Age of Anxiety*. The process we are dealing with was already at work in the early Greek world, in the transformation which Dodds called the change from the "shame culture" to the "guilt culture" (*The Greeks and the Irrational*, p. 28ff.).

account of the movements seeking to counter it. The early empire desperately tried to revive primitive Roman cults in a fundamentalist (let's have the old-time religion) crusade. Men longed for the good old days, for the world of corn and blood and wine and water. The cynic-stoic philosophers stood on corners of decumanus and cardo and preached ethical diatribes as substitutes for religious laws. A bizarre conglomeration of mythological fragments, strewn through Hermetic and Gnostic systems, in artificially fabricated cosmogonies, are witnesses to the chaos of organic mythic traditions. Uneasiness about the loss of the mythological world did not disappear; reactions to that loss grew from the age of Augustus to that of Diocletian. How deeply the mythological crisis had caused fear and insecurity among the population also can be measured by the fury with which the Roman mob reacted when Christians were accused of being "atheists" and by the success of Neoplatonic philosophy, in which Platonic and Aristotelian concepts were definitely "theologized." The very fact that practically every one of these responses to the mythological crisis contained strong dualistic, either asexual or overtly antisexual, elements demonstrates the relationship between the loss of religious mythological safety and the loss of sexual identity.[42] It is therefore no coincidence that the second-century movement which so desperately tried to recover the mythological canopy, namely Gnosticism, picked Gen. 3, the idea of a fall, as the starting point for its remythologization in which sexual copulation belongs to heaven, as an abstract cosmic event beyond human reach. Nor is it a coincidence that the philosophical parallel to Gnosticism, middle Platonism by Numenius and his followers, declared body and matter as evil. When man began to lose his secure place in the mythic-cosmic structure which he had hewn for himself,

42. The best examples are the Jewish antisexual texts (*Hen. aeg.* 32; Julius Gross, *Entstehungsgeschichte des Erbsündendogmas* [Munich and Basel, 1960], pp. 38ff.); the Gnostic and apocryphal docetic documents (*Exc. ex Theod.* 21.1–2; *Evang. Thom.* 80); the *Manual of Discipline;* the exclusive male character of the Mithraic house community that assembled in a cave (Thomas Freedam, *art. cit.*). On the powerful appeal of the secret cult, see A. D. Nock, *Conversion* (New York, 1932), pp. 99ff. On the psychological problem of ancient man leading to mystic sublimation, see A. J. Festugière, *Hermétisme et mystique païenne* (Paris, 1967), pp. 13ff.

he was thrown into a crisis. Perhaps he lost his place because he became urban, and thus conscious of man's universal predicament. No matter what caused this crisis, the bishops and presbyters of Elvira, as the leaders of an exclusive religion, offered an alternative which reckoned with the sexual dilemma of their age.

Five

A POSTSCRIPT:
ELVIRA AND VATICAN II

Sixteen and a half centuries after the council of Elvira, the Second Vatican Council assembled in Rome. In the long list of Christian synods from which we have written decisions, Elvira is the earliest and Vaticanum Secundum is the most recent. I close my book on Elvira by drawing certain parallels between these two councils which span a fascinating epoch in history: the first opened Christianity's Constantinian period, the second played its coda. Comparing these two assemblies, I mean to point out how both of them took place in a moment of acute change and, hence, of crisis within the church; how the very enterprise of each council consisted in coping with such crisis; and how the modern council, although significantly repudiating the former's trends on certain matters, perpetuated Elvira's tragic mistakes on others, trying to redeem the church's hatred of Jews and heretics, but not daring to open the explosive and yet so crucial issues of hierarchy, celibacy and sexuality. From the dynamic of a contemporary event, it was proposed at the outset, one can learn something about a past synod; concomitantly, from the analysis of the past one can throw light on the modern event.

There are many arresting parallels between the two councils. They both took place in a church, the first in *ecclesia Eliberitana,* which must have been a simple, pre-Constantine basilica-like structure; the second in San Pietro, that vast Renaissance temple, standing on the Vatican hill, crowned by Michelangelo's superb cupola. Center stage in both were the church leaders, bishops and presbyters handing down canonical judgments in the first; cardinals and bishops deliberating schemata in the second, while the church at large waited and watched, audience only. At Elvira, deacons and the people stood by, as Mansi's text reports; at Vatican II not only the Catholic, but also surprisingly large segments of the non-Catholic world observed through the news media. The numbers and the character of the two synods differed vastly. While at Elvira there were nineteen bishops and twenty-six presbyters, primarily from the southern part of the Iberian peninsula, at the Vatican there were 2,500 bishops and cardinals from all over the world. At Elvira was a small provincial assembly, composing its canons in crude Latin, betraying its literary limitations; at Vatican II a splendid group of clerics flying from all nations to the Leonardo da Vinci Airport in order to draw up schemata couched in sophisticated theological language, making use of both a rich heritage of two thousand years of theological speculations and erudite twentieth-century scholarship. The decision-making processes differed. The canons of Elvira were arrived at through a spontaneous and fresh group process, while the schemata of Vatican II were conceived, debated, and polished in committees and preliminary meetings and finally approved in plenary sessions in the nave of Saint Peter's.

But in both councils the symptoms of change, the evidences of crisis are unmistakable. The council of Elvira marked the transformation of an aggressive sectarian movement to an imperial cult religion, and that transformation produced, as the canons show, a great deal of ambivalence. The Second Vaticanum occurred when patristic-medieval Catholicism found itself finally confronted by the modern world, and large amounts of ferment, long damned up in the church and unknown only to the outsider, surfaced. Both Elvira and Vatican II reveal that profound changes were going on in what was at the time traditional Catholic religion: at Elvira the final surrender of the primitive eschatological sect, at the Vatican the collapse of the medieval cult religion that had seen its apex so many centuries before. The protesting conservative cardinals saw quite clearly that the liberal representatives of the Vatican council were willing to terminate, without always realizing the full implications, an entire epoch of Catholicism. The church, however, had no choice. A religion changes only under immense external pressures, and the Second Vaticanum was centuries overdue. What went on in Rome in the early 1960s was by no means a sudden storm unleashed by a few eccentrics. Just as the synod of Elvira met, with all its sharp conflicts between anticultural exclusive and pro-imperial inclusive factions of Christianity, because the church had to respond to the pressures for change, so the Second Vatican, that test between conservative and liberal factions in Catholicism, went on its cautious and yet, for some, so radical course because the time was ripe. It was overripe.

The two crises have in common that they were both produced by rapid secularization. The difference between secular and religious, or sacred, is historical. The religious community determines what is sacred. Frequently, the secular of one age becomes the sacred of another. In turn, what at one time flourishes as sacred custom or thought will finally exist or terminate as secular. What people call secularization is the last stage of the process in which either the cultic organization adapts to its context or in which certain sacred phenomena are given back to, or are acknowledged in, a noncultic use. Take the issue of Latin in the liturgy, raised by Vatican II. For the churches of Elvira, Latin as used in the liturgy and in the canons was the ordinary language of the people; fides, templum, fecerit, crimen, the words of can. 1 belonged to everyday life in Baetica, and placuit cunctis could have been said the same day by a municipal senate in Merida or Italica. For the churches of Elvira, Latin was not sacred in the sense it became so in modern Catholicism. It was not the language of the great sacred past distinct from the language of contemporary culture. To be analogous the liturgy of Spain would have had to be celebrated in Hebrew or in New Testament Greek. The surrender of liturgical Latin, as advocated by a majority of bishops in Vatican II, acknowledged that for dynamic Catholicism Latin as a linguistic symbol of an exclusive community and as a linguistic tool for political unity had to be given up; it had become archaic. *Romanitas,* the secret behind Elvira's transformations, had lost its momentum by the time of Vatican II.

As to the issue of Christianity's relation to power and secular culture, in the council of Elvira one of the major crises was due to the church's adaptation to the secular, imperial-antique context, its transformation into an imperial cult institution. To be sure, this transformation of the primitive Christian eschatological sect began before the apostolic age was over, but the crucial secularization took place right after Elvira: exemption from taxes, brilliant sanctuaries, state support, mass conversions. The Second Vaticanum showed Catholicism in the process of seeing the collapse of precisely those structures for which the council of Elvira had fought. The patristic-medieval forms of thought and organization, the vertical authoritarian models of theology, ethic and hierarchy, so basic to the fourth and consecutive centuries of the Christian church, are challenged and replaced by new social and intellectual models considerably more democratic and much more understanding of the interrelation between man and woman, leader and follower, intellectual and worker. In both of these councils a crisis was inevitable because the traditional patterns and models were given up only partly, and then only under pressure. The crisis was heightened because secularization was not only incomplete but tended to destroy, in the eyes of many devout believers, the historically established character of the church.

On two issues, as has been indicated, Vatican II repudiated by significant actions tragic attitudes and positions directly promulgated in the canons of Elvira, namely the repressive treatment of Jews and the hostility toward heretics. In prohibiting all intermarriage with Jews, the blessing of crops by Jews, or even the sharing of meals with Jews— all that pathetic bigotry for the sake of Christian arcaneness—the ancient synod codified the kernels of a fatal anti-Semitism which justified the use of a Jew as scapegoat on whom the Christian could always unload his frustration and against whom the threatened Christian community could purge and consolidate itself by sacrifice, pogrom, crusade. I do not imply that Jews were persecuted in Spain at that time. We have no evidence to verify that, although we have no evidence to the contrary either. But the pattern was set. It led to medieval anti-Semitic terror, the burning of Jews on an island in the Rhine river during the first crusade, to Luther's venomous phrases against them, to the most recent outbursts of anti-Semitism in Germany and the United States, in Poland and the Soviet Union. After all, to the paranoid among Christians, and among their contemporary secular followers, the Jew was the murderer of God.

Some Jews, not comprehending the pervasiveness of that paranoia, have been incensed that anyone should be congratulatory about Vatican Council's reconciling remarks toward Israel. After all, they say, should it have taken intelligent, redeemed, loving Christian men so long to become aware of their incredible bigotry? Should not the pronouncements of Vatican II have been affirmed by the ancient church? Of course they should have, but asking the question is futile rhetoric, betraying ignorance of the absurd irrationality in historical evolution. Why do we sometimes learn only at age forty what we should have known at age fourteen? Why did the Second Vaticanum perform, and only reluctantly at that, the task the church should have performed a century or more before? What the Jewish question does point to, however, is the depth of the anti-Semitic problem in Christian history. When the leaders at Vatican II dared to make their so long delayed ecclesiastical apology about the Christian church's traditional hostility toward the Jews, they set out to deal with Christian guilt and thereby to become free of the church's tragic past. Bloodshed, agony, injustice, and murder had been visited on millions of people because of Christian anti-Semitism. Near the Theater of Marcellus stands the church of Sant' Angelo in Pescheria where for hundreds of years Jews were forced to attend mass, a mass in which they did not believe and which they had to endure with pain. It is that crime against human integrity, committed in the name of Christian salvation, that Rolf Hochhuth's *Vicar* reveals. As in American racism, a declaration of guilt does not solve the problem, but it is a first step toward making the community conscious of the problem, toward naming the guilt and thereby, perhaps, beginning to expiate it. On that count, the Catholic church is struggling to come of age.

But the Vatican Council's redemptive statements vis-à-vis Judaism have a second implication. A new movement in history has to express its newness through polemical models by which it can distinguish itself from its roots, its predecessors. Primitive Christianity identified itself as the "new covenant," the "new Israel," implying: "our uniqueness." The two beautiful sculptures at the south portal of Strassburg Cathedral define the church's notion of its identity and its role: Ecclesia is a queen, beautifully robed, holding the chalice and the victorious cross; Synagoga, blindfolded and sad, holds the broken staff. When the Second Vatican Council made a special effort to rectify its relationship with the Jews, it not only committed an act of reconciliation, but it acknowledged that its ideological separation from Judaism, its construction of old and new covenant, its attempt to create an artificial gap between church and synagogue, between believer and unbeliever, had been absorbed into history. Primitive Christianity, like the Gothic sculpture at Strassburg, saw the Jew as misled, blind, stubborn, an unbeliever, or perhaps at best waiting, prophesying, and pointing toward full truth. The nascent reconciliation with the Jews by the Christian church is, whether or not fully comprehended as such by the fathers of the council, an admission that the juxtaposition of Abraham and Christ (Rom. 5) reflects an historical social conflict. What sounds to many like a long overdue document on religious toleration turns out in fact to be a document which will require the church in the future to define its uniqueness differently from its past model of promise and fulfillment.

Just as the contemporary church's position in regard to the Jews is a sign that a reassessment of its past is inescapable, so its position toward non-Catholic churches implies an equally radical reorientation of the Catholic church's place in contemporary pluralism, both religious and cultural. For the fathers of the council of Elvira, pluralism was heresy, to be prevented at all costs, a sin, a breach of the Christian church's claim to be *una, sancta, catholica,* and *apostolica.* For over fifteen hundred years, Catholicism has operated with this artificial construct of orthodoxy and heresy in order to define its character and to build up its strength. The terms are relative, of course, and shifting, for just as the sacred becomes the secular, and the secular becomes the sacred, so the heretic of one age becomes the orthodox of another, and vice-versa. "We are orthodox" means: we are right and you are wrong. "You are a heretic" means: we don't like what you say, in the first place because your thoughts are too threatening to us at the moment, and in the second place because we need strict authoritarian beliefs in order to preserve our security. Without an orthodox there is no heretic, but, also, there is no heretic unless the orthodox creates him.

In Vatican II the concept of heresy no longer appears. Such omission may seem at first sight merely a minor detail, accidental, but it is not. The schema *De Ecclesia* is beginning to give up the heretic as the construed enemy of the church, and this change implies that Catholicism surrenders a traditional device for safeguarding its identity, daring to contemplate survival without making its brother churches into foes. The change was dramatically exemplified in the fact that the Vatican invited non-Catholic observers to its sessions. I sat one afternoon in a room of the Columbus Hotel, only a few steps from Saint Peter's, and watched Catholic bishops discuss one of their schemata with Methodist, Reformed, Anglican, and Orthodox theologians, and I became aware for the first time of what profound changes were taking place among Catholicism's elite. This willingness—deplored, to be sure, by an entire segment of the church, and understandably so—to open up the Catholic exclusivity to the plurality of the Christian world and thereby to take seriously the horizontal-relative-historical level of truth, will bring along, without any doubt, a redefinition of what thus far has continued to be patristic and medieval Catholic Christianity. When a church gives up the heretic, it gives up its orthodoxy.

While in issues like these, Vatican II broke with its two thousand-year-old tradition, in other issues it failed, and totally so, to come to terms with its past. This failure lay, above all, in the council's reluctance to acknowledge the obsolescence of its traditional structures of authority, an obsolescence that is directly related to the more and more open avowel of the role of sexuality in religious communities as well as in the society at large.

As I have shown, the decisions of Elvira were made from a premise of a hierarchic social structure of life that was basic to both the ancient church and the ancient world. This "elite" consciousness from which the canons were pronounced belongs to the late antique world: the leader is always far above, the follower is always far below, neither consulted nor allowed to share in the decision-making process. *Ubi episcopus, ibi ecclesia* resulted naturally from the vertical pattern of authority in the Roman Empire. What was good for the bishop had to be good for the church; whatever the layman sought in the Christian community depended on what the leader wanted him to find. The relationship between bishop/presbyter and faithful was one of dependence and domination. The cleric saw himself in the role of the powerful father, alternately punishing and forgiving, as the analysis of the decision patterns of Elvira has shown. The faithful looked up, or was conditioned to look up to him as his paternal authority figure, his "papa," as the major bishops since the third century were called. Such a vertical relationship, elsewhere expressed as lord-servant, teacher-student, undergirds the entire patristic and medieval authority structure of Christianity, as one of the two components in the mother-father substitute presented to man by the ancient church. While the church offered itself to the believer as the spiritual mother who comforts and nourishes her children, the elite of the church acted as the father, distributing wrath and clemency in the gratuitous, manipulative technique of autocratic power.

The often-presented view which sees the patristic church as episcopal and therefore relatively democratic and closer to egalitarian models, and the medieval church as papal and thus less democratic, misses entirely the authority problem as posed by both Elvira and Vatican II. Actually, leadership in the ancient church had two aspects, closely related to each other: one being individual-autocratic and the other collegiate-aristocratic. The individual-autocratic pattern functioned from the very beginning of the ecclesiastical development. Ignatius of Antioch saw himself presiding over the church as bishop, just as Jesus ruled over the apostles. As the church grew, the autocratic authority of bishops grew, more in major cities than in minor towns. The evolution of metropolitan powers, ambiguously dealt with at the council of Elvira (58), was at work in every individual province and culminated in the creation of two patriarchal-papal powers, Constantinople and Rome. Parallel to this individual-autocratic pattern, a collegiate type of leadership emerged in two steps: first, in the early Christian trifold office of deacon, presbyter, and bishop, with the bishop, of course, as the highest, and second, in an episcopal body of bishops—in Elvira it was a body of bishops and presbyters—meeting in provincial and imperial councils at Carthage, Arles, Nicaea, Ephesus, Constantinople. All of these authority patterns were antique-authoritarian-paternalistic-vertical. The much-applauded return to collegiality announced by the Second Vaticanum is, therefore, neither revolutionary nor particularly liberalizing. What it amounts to is a limitation of individual autocracy, not in favor of greater participation by the church but of greater power by the clerical elite. This shift stays within the antique scheme of human relationship and ignores totally the context of twentieth-century life, which prescribes horizontal patterns of authority very different from those vertical ones basic to the ancient world. There was not a single layman nor one woman deciding on a single issue in the nave of St. Peter's. The "return" to collegiality ignores the leadership forms which have been evolving in contemporary cultures and which demand a total change of ecclesiastical authority: models of communal decision-making, of the democratic process, of interaction between leadership and constituency choosing this leadership, of rotating leadership.

The failure to consider such new models and, hence, to prepare the church for a radical retreat from its hierarchic scaffold is rooted in the abortiveness of the Vatican synod's confrontation with the issue of sexuality. The council vaunted its dialogue with the modern world; yet, in the most pressing of modern matters—birth control, contraception, priestly celibacy, divorce—despite a few attempts, it failed. Why, one must ask, did the pope kill the birth-control issue by taking it away from the council and giving it over to Cardinal Ottaviani, so proud of being the eleventh of twelve children? How is it that the prelates in the Città del Vaticano could ignore a major contemporary phenomenon, the open sensuality expressed by the thousands and tens of thousands of men and women who flock to the beaches of Ostia and Anzio? How could the elite of the Vatican ignore so resolutely Italy's major artistic contributions to the contemporary scene, the films of Fellini, Rossellini, or Antonioni, or the novels of Silone and Moravia? One must ask the question in terms of the church's primary function: how dare a church, part of whose task is to heal, to council, to guide in crises, and to give hope in moments of frustration and guilt, imagine it can perform its task constructively or even realistically, if not to say rationally, without meeting the challenges of psychological insights into the human personality?

The explanation for this ostrich-like reticence to modify its traditional stance is quite clear. As has been shown, the establishment of clerical control in the patristic church was tied closely to a strong control of, actually a limitation on, the sexual behavior of the faithful and to the creation of an ascetic ideal by which such control could be supported and enforced. To change the sexual teaching of the church, still sustained by an ideal of an unmarried clerical elite and by a dominant-dependent order in human relationship, would mean to shake the very power structure of that church. Despite some attempts, Vatican II did not come to terms with the contemporary sexual revolution because the issue was too dangerous. For the church to change its positions on sexual behavior and ideals weakens traditional authority, and such a transformation would have immense economic as well as psychological implications. Such transformation would change not only the structure of the parish and the image of the priest, but it would mean basic changes in doctrine on sin, fall, and salvation, on the development and character of the human personality, on ethical freedom, on infant baptism, and on the nature of justice and social action. Of course such changes in teaching have been advocated in books and journals. I believe that the conservative cardinals must have known all too well that the age of Elvira was over. Yet, at the council the changes were verbalized only reluctantly and guardedly, if at all. One item tells the whole story: while on most decisions, the liberal, or what seems a somewhat liberal, majority was significant, on the issue of an exceedingly cautious liberalizing of mariological statements there no longer was an overwhelming liberal majority.

How liberal then was Vatican II? The question cannot be answered with a simple formula. The newest Catholic synod was an event in which progressive and conservative ideas were pitched against each other by clerics, the majority of whom had a somewhat progressive tendency, but who were not even at the same stage of historical evolution. There was a general liberalizing mood in the council, which generated a feeling of newness so characteristic of moments of crucial mutations in the historical process. This newness, however, despite the pride of many of the council members, was not akin to daring. Only some of the bishops were liberal, and only some of the time, on some of the issues. The patterns and models of their interactions were complicated and ambiguous, wrung out of tradition and old positions that were affected by the debates in the council itself, but not necessarily metamorphosed into viable new forms. The schemata of Vatican II are not one iota less complex, pluralistic, or confused than the decisions of Elvira which I have analyzed. Like Elvira, Vatican II should be analyzed as process rather than result, as fragments of conflicts and interaction rather than as clear position statements. In its demand for *aggiornamento* the council tampered with the very foundations of the Catholic traditional church, but in its decisions it did not dare to carry out its demand. It took Constantine, with his political acumen and his monomaniacal belief in his own historical role, undergirded by fabricated miracles and the bishops' shrewd support, to carry out what a majority of Elvira's participants had envisaged. I do not know what it will take to lead the world of Vatican II into a Catholicism that deals positively with the democratic process and the dynamic of the human personality.

THE CANONS

The critical edition of the Canons of Elvira, announced several years ago, has not yet been published. My translation, which attempts to keep the character of the primitive Latin original, is based primarily on the Hefele text in its French, Leclercq form, which goes back to Gonzalez. The new Spanish text, J. Vives, T. Martin, and G. Martinez, *Concilios visigoticos e hispano-romanos* (Barcelona and Madrid, 1963) vol. 1, does not offer a critical analysis of the manuscripts and does not suffice as a basis for research.

Can. 1. It is decided that anyone of a mature age, who, after the faith of saving baptism, approaches a temple as an idolater and commits this major crime, because it is an enormity of the highest order, is not to receive communion even at the end.

Can. 2. Flamines who, after the faith of font and regeneration, have sacrificed, since they have thereby doubled their crimes by adding murder, or even tripled their evil deed by including sexual offense, are not to receive communion even at the end.

Can. 3. At the same time, flamines who have not actually sacrificed but simply performed their function may, since they have refrained from the deadly sacrifices, be offered communion at the end, provided that the required penance has been done. If, however, after the penance they commit a sexual offense, it is decided to accord them no further communion, lest they seem to make a mockery of the Sunday communion.

Can. 4. Again, flamines who are catechumens and who have refrained from sacrifices shall be admitted after a period of three years.

Can. 5. If a woman overcome with rage whips her maidservant so badly that she dies within three days, and it is doubtful whether she killed her on purpose or by accident: provided that the required penance has been done, she shall be readmitted after seven years, if it was done purposely, and after five years if accidentally; in the event that she becomes ill during the set time, let her receive communion.

Can. 6. If anyone kills another by sorcery, communion is not to be given to him even at the end, since he could not have accomplished this crime without idolatry.

Can. 7. If one of the faithful, after a sexual offense and after the required period of penance, should again commit fornication, he shall not have communion even at the end.

Can. 8. Again, women who, without any preceding cause, leave their husbands and take up with other men are not to receive communion even at the end.

Can. 9. Further, a baptized woman who leaves her adulterous baptized husband and marries another is forbidden to marry him; if she does she shall not receive communion until the death of her former husband unless, by chance, the pressure of illness demand that it be given.

Can. 10. If a woman who has been deserted by her catechumen husband marries another man, she may be admitted to the font of baptism; this also applies to female catechumens. But if the man who leaves the innocent woman marries a Christian woman, and this woman knew he had a wife whom he had left without cause, communion may be given to her at death.

Can. 11. If that female catechumen should grow seriously ill during the five-year period, baptism is not to be denied her.

Can. 12. A mother or female guardian or any Christian woman who engages in pandering, since she is selling another's body—or even her own —she shall not receive communion even at the end.

Can. 13. Virgins who have consecrated themselves to God, if they break their vow of virginity and turn to lust instead, not realizing what they lose, shall not be given communion at the end. If, however, corrupted by the fall of their weak body only once, they do penance for the rest of their lives, and abstain from intercourse so that they only seem fallen, they may receive communion at the end.

Can. 14. Virgins who have not preserved their virginity, if they marry those who violated them and keep them as husband, they must be reconciled without penance after a year since they have broken only the nuptials. If, however, they have been intimate with other men—becoming guilty of real sexual offense—they ought to be admitted to communion only after five years, having fulfilled the required penance.

Can. 15. No matter the large number of girls, Christian maidens are by no means to be given in matrimony to pagans lest youth, bursting forth in bloom, end in adultery of the soul.

Can. 16. Heretics, if they are unwilling to change over to the Catholic church, are not to have Catholic girls given to them in marriage, nor shall they be given to Jews or heretics, since there can be no community for the faithful with the unfaithful. If parents act against this prohibition, they shall be kept out for five years.

Can. 17. If any should perchance join their daughters in marriage to priests of the idols, they shall not be given communion even at the end.

Can. 18. Bishops, presbyters, and deacons, if—once placed in the ministry —they are discovered to be sexual offenders, shall not receive communion, not even at the end, because of the scandal and the heinousness of the crime.

Can. 19. Bishops, presbyters, and deacons are not to abandon their territories for commercial reasons, nor shall they run around the provinces seeking after profitable business; in order to procure their livelihood, let them rather send a son or freedman, an employee, a friend, or whomever they want; if they want to pursue business, let them do it within their own province.

Can. 20. If anyone of the clergy has been discovered practicing usury, he shall be degraded and kept away. If a layman, too, is shown to have practiced usury and, after having been accused, promises to stop and no longer to exact interest, he shall be granted pardon; if, however, he should persist in this wickedness, he is to be cast out of the church.

Can. 21. If anyone living in the city does not go to church for three Sundays, he shall be kept out for a short time in order that his punishment be made public.

Can. 22. If anyone goes over from the Catholic church to heresy and returns again, penance shall not be denied to him since he has recognized his sin. He shall do penance for ten years, and after these ten years, communion shall be offered to him. If, however, as children they were carried away, they shall be received back without delay since they have not sinned on their own.

Can. 23. The extensions of the fast shall be celebrated through each month —except for the days of the two months of July and August, because of some people's weakness.

Can. 24. All those who have been baptized away from home, since their life has scarcely been examined, shall not be promoted to the clergy in foreign provinces.

Can. 25. Anyone who carries a letter of a confessor should be given instead a letter of communion eliminating the title "confessor," since all those sharing in the glory of this title at times upset the simple people.

Can. 26. In order to correct the erroneous practice, it is decided that we must celebrate the extension of the fast every Saturday.

Can. 27. A bishop or any other cleric may have living with him only a sister or a virgin daughter dedicated to God; by no means shall he keep any woman unrelated to him.

Can. 28. A bishop shall not take a gift from one who is not in communion.

Can. 29. A possessed man who is tormented by an erratic spirit shall not have his name read out at the altar with the offering; nor shall he be permitted to serve personally in the church.

Can. 30. Those who in their youth have sinned sexually are not to be ordained subdeacons inasmuch as they might afterwards be promoted by deception to a higher order. Furthermore, if any have been ordained in the past, they are to be removed.

Can. 31. Young men who after the faith of saving baptism have committed sexual offense shall be admitted to communion when they marry, provided the required penance is done.

Can. 32. If anyone, through grave sin, has fallen into fatal ruin, he shall not do penance before a presbyter but rather before the bishop; however, under the pressure of illness it is necessary that a presbyter shall offer communion, and even a deacon if a priest orders him.

Can. 33. Bishops, presbyters, and deacons and all other clerics having a position in the ministry are ordered to abstain completely from their wives and not to have children. Whoever, in fact, does this, shall be expelled from the dignity of the clerical state.

Can. 34. Candles shall not be burned in a cemetery during the day, for the spirits of the saints are not to be disturbed. Those who do not observe this are excluded from the communion of the church.

Can. 35. Women are forbidden to spend the night in a cemetery since often under the pretext of prayer they secretly commit evil deeds.

Can. 36. There shall be no pictures in churches, lest what is worshipped and adored be depicted on walls.

Can. 37. Those who are tormented by unclean spirits, if they have reached the point of death, shall be baptized; if they are already baptized, communion shall be given them. Furthermore, these people are forbidden to light candles publicly. If they want to act against the prohibition, they shall be kept away from communion.

Can. 38. On the occasion of a trip or if a church is not near, a baptized Christian who has kept his baptism intact and who is not married a second time can baptize a catechumen who is critically ill, as long as he takes him to the bishop if he survives, so that it can be completed through the laying on of hands.

Can. 39. Pagans, if in sickness they wish to have the laying on of hands, and if their life has been at least partially decent, shall have the laying on of hands and become Christians.

Can. 40. It is forbidden that landholders, when they receive their payments, shall account as received anything offered to idols. If after this prohibition they do so anyway, they shall be severed from communion for the space of five years.

Can. 41. The faithful are warned to forbid, as far as they can, that idols be kept in their homes. If, however, they fear violence from their slaves, they must at least keep themselves pure. If they do not do this, they are to be considered outside the church.

Can. 42. Those who arrive at the first stage of faith, if their reputation has been good, shall be admitted to the grace of baptism in two ·years, unless under the pressure of illness reason compels help more rapidly for the one approaching death or at least the one begging for grace.

Can. 43. The perverted custom shall be changed in accordance with the authority of the scriptures, so that we all celebrate the day of Pentecost, lest anyone who does not conform be regarded as having introduced a new heresy.

Can. 44. A prostitute who once lived as such and later married, if afterwards she has come to belief, shall be received without delay.

Can. 45. As for one who was a catechumen and for a long time did not go to church at all, if one of the clergy acknowledged him to be a Christian, or if some of the faithful come forward as witnesses, baptism shall not be denied him since he appears to have cast off the old man.

Can. 46. If one of the faithful, having forsaken his religion, has not come to church for a long time but should then return, as long as he has not been an idolater, he shall receive communion after ten years.

Can. 47. If a baptized married man commits adultery, not once but often, he is to be approached at the hour of death. If he promises to stop, communion shall be given him; if he should recover and commit adultery again, he shall nevermore make a mockery of the communion of peace.

Can. 48. The custom of placing coins in the baptismal shell by those being baptized must be corrected so that the priest does not seem to sell for money what he has received freely. Nor shall their feet be washed by priests or clerics.

Can. 49. Landholders are warned not to allow the crops, which they have received from God with an act of thanksgiving, to be blessed by Jews lest they make our blessing ineffectual and weak. If anyone dares to do this after the prohibition, he shall be thrown out of the church completely.

Can. 50. If any of the clergy or the faithful eats with Jews, he shall be kept from communion in order that he be corrected as he should.

Can. 51. If a baptized person has come from any heresy, by no means is he to be promoted to the clergy; if any have been ordained in the past, they shall be deposed without any question.

Can. 52. Those who have been caught placing derogatory writings in church shall be anathematized.

Can. 53. It is agreed by all that a person is to receive communion from that bishop by whom he was denied it for a particular crime. If another bishop presumes to admit him without the participation or consent of the bishop by whom he was deprived of communion, let him know that in this way he is going to create cause for dissent among the brethren and bring danger to his own position.

Can. 54. If parents break the betrothal agreement, they shall be kept away for three years. But if either the groom or the bride has been caught in a serious crime, the parents are excused. If, however, the sin was mutual and the betrothed have defiled each other, the former penalty holds.

Can. 55. Priests who simply wear the wreath and who neither sacrifice nor offer any of their income to idols shall receive communion after two years.

Can. 56. A magistrate is ordered to keep away from the church during the one year of his term as duumvir.

Can. 57. Matrons or their husbands are not to lend their finery to enhance a procession in a worldly fashion, and if they do so, they are to be kept away for three years.

Can. 58. We have resolved that everywhere, and especially where the principal episcopal chair has been established, those who present letters of communion shall be interrogated to determine whether everything is verified by their testimony.

Can. 59. It is forbidden for any Christian to go up to the idol of the capitol, as a pagan does in order to sacrifice, and watch. If he does, he is guilty of the same crime. If he was baptized, he may be received, having completed his penance, after ten years.

Can. 60. If someone has broken idols and on that account was put to death, inasmuch as this is not written in the Gospel nor is it found ever to have been done in the time of the apostles, he shall not be included in the ranks of the martyrs.

Can. 61. If a man after the death of his wife marries her sister and she was baptized, he shall be kept away from communion for five years, unless perchance the pressure of illness demands that peace be given more quickly.

Can. 62. If a charioteer or pantomime wants to believe, they shall first renounce their professions and only then be accepted on the condition that they do not later return to their former professions; if they attempt to violate this decision, they shall be expelled from the church.

Can. 63. If a woman, while her husband is away, conceives by adultery and after that crime commits abortion, she shall not be given communion even at the end, since she has doubled her crime.

Can. 64. If a woman remains in adultery with another man up to the end of her life, she shall not be given communion even at the end. But if she should leave him, she may receive communion after ten years, having completed the required penance.

Can. 65. If the wife of a cleric has committed adultery, and her husband knew of it but did not immediately throw her out, he shall not receive communion even at the end, lest it appear as though instruction in crime is coming from those who should be the model of a good life.

Can. 66. If a man marries his step-daughter, inasmuch as he is incestuous, he shall not be given communion even at the end.

Can. 67. It is forbidden for a woman, whether baptized or a catechumen, to have anything to do with long-haired men or hairdressers; any who do this shall be kept from communion.

Can. 68. A catechumen, if she has conceived a child in adultery and then suffocated it, shall be baptized at the end.

Can. 69. If a married man happens to fall once, he shall do penance for a period of five years and thus be reconciled, unless the pressure of illness compels that communion be given before that time: this is also binding for women.

Can. 70. If a wife, with her husband's knowledge, has committed adultery, he shall not be given communion even at the end; but if he gets rid of her, he may receive communion after ten years, if he kept her in his home for any length of time once he knew of the adultery.

Can. 71. Men who sexually abuse boys shall not be given communion even at the end.

Can. 72. If a widow has intercourse with a man and later marries him, she shall be reconciled to communion after a period of five years, having completed the required penance; if she marries another man, having left the first, she shall not be given communion even at the end; however, if the man she marries is one of the faithful, she shall not receive communion except after ten years, having completed the required penance, unless illness compels that communion be given more quickly.

Can. 73. An informer, if he was baptized and through his denunciation some one was proscribed or killed, shall not receive communion even at the end; if it was a lesser case, he can receive communion within five years; if the informer was a catechumen, he may be admitted to baptism after a period of five years.

Can. 74. A false witness since he has committed a crime shall be kept away; but if what he brought about did not lead to death and he has explained satisfactorily why he did not keep silent, he shall be kept away for a period of two years; however, if he cannot prove this to the assembly of the clergy, he shall be excluded for five years.

Can. 75. If anyone attacks a bishop, presbyter, or deacon by accusing them of false crimes, and he is unable to prove them, communion shall not be given him even at the end.

Can. 76. If someone allows himself to be ordained deacon, and afterwards is discovered in a mortal crime, which he had committed at one time: if he confessed on his own, he shall receive communion after three years, having completed the required penance; but if someone else exposes him, he shall receive lay communion after five years, having done his penance.

Can. 77. If a deacon in charge of common people with no bishop or presbyter baptizes some of them, the bishop shall perfect them by his blessing; but if they leave this world before that, a man can be regarded as justified depending on the faith by which he believed.

Can. 78. If one of the faithful who is married commits adultery with a Jewish or a pagan woman, he shall be cut off, but if some one else exposes him, he can share Sunday communion after five years, having completed the required penance.

Can. 79. If one of the faithful plays dice, that is, on a playing board, for money, he shall be kept away; if, having reformed, he stops, he may be reconciled to communion after a year.

Can. 80. It is forbidden for freedmen whose former masters are still alive to be promoted to the clergy.

Can. 81. Women shall not presume on their own, without their husbands' signatures, to write to lay women who are baptized, nor shall they accept anyone's letters of peace addressed only to themselves.

INDEX

Abbott, E.F., 71
Abortion, 48, 50, 88, 98, 99
Abstinere, 41
Actiones, 20
Adultery, 13, 40, 43, 48, 60, 88–93, 101, 104, 106
Ambiguity, 5, 7, 8, 17–19, 34–38, 43–44, 54, 72, 74, 84, 88, 97, 99, 115
Ambrose, 82
Amos, 111
Analogy. *See* Methodology
Anathema, 22, 25, 28, 30, 38, 39, 46, 53, 54, 58, 60, 94, 98
Anti-Semitism, 82, 117–18
Apocrypha, 107, 112
Apostasy, 11, 12, 13, 48, 58, 60, 86, 89
Apostolic constitution, 82
Apostolic tradition, 85, 99
Arbitrariness, 12, 13, 29, 33, 45, 49, 51, 57, 66, 74, 99
Arcaneness, 50, 54, 80, 87, 104, 109–12, 117, 120
Arceri, 39–40
Arnobius, 81
Art, 35, 36, 105, 106, 110, 111
Asceticism, 87, 95, 100, 101, 104, 105, 123; and social reality, 101. *See also* Celibacy; Monasticism; Virgins
Assemblies, 69–71; concilia, 63, 70, 71; provincial, 70–71; collegia, 70, 79. *See also* Councils; Flamines
Athanasius, 77, 100, 104

Augustine, 54, 84, 89, 103
Augustus, 63, 87, 112
Aurelian, 68

Bacchanalia Trial, 72
Baetica, 8, 65, 66, 73, 78, 79, 81, 85, 87, 116
Baptism, 20, 31, 39, 41, 48–50, 61, 64, 78, 84, 85, 123
Batiffol, P., 11
Belief, 5, 62, 83, 92, 93, 101
Berger, A., 26
Bishops, 6, 11, 19, 31, 32, 37, 41, 44, 50, 62–81, 86–88, 100, 121–22; authority, 3, 19, 25, 27, 29, 36, 37, 68; and presbyters, 11, 57, 67; priestly function, 49; at Vaticanum II, 121–22. *See also* Conflict; Decision, decision-making process; Elite
Bouchier, E.S., 68, 79
Buddhism, 107

Caldo, A., 79
Canon: complexity, 18, 81; inconsistency, 5, 12, 45, 49; nature of, 4, 8, 27, 41, 45, 54, 56, 59, 86, 124; sequence, 11, 32, 33, 44, 46, 58, 59; spontaneity, 11, 12, 14, 25, 32, 33, 44, 46, 49, 58, 112; uncertainty, 14, 26, 38, 45, 54, 73. *See also* Decision, decision-making process; Language; Law

Pentecost, 31

Persecution, 53, 63, 87, 112, 117

Petersen, H., 70

Philo, 111

Philosophy, 35, 60, 105, 107, 108, 109, 112

Pidal, R., 110

Placuit, 10, 13, 26, 27, 48

Pliny, 10, 78

Plotinus, 105, 109, 112

Plumpe, J.C., 107

Pluralism, 108, 109, 119, 120

Popular Christianity, 36, 81

Popular religion, 34

Possessores, 42, 58, 69, 75, 77

Power, 18, 51, 64, 69, 81, 90, 121

Presbyters, 6, 11, 19, 67, 74, 77, 88, 122

Priscillian, 54, 83

Prostitution, 31, 85, 88, 98, 99

Province, 54, 57, 63, 66, 68–70, 75–79, 87, 102, 108–9

Prudentius, 87

Quintillian, 60, 63

Quispel, 106

Redemptive community, 66, 81, 84, 113, 123

Resurrection, 50–51

Revolution, 61

Roman Empire, 15, 56, 58, 63, 64, 65, 69, 70, 72, 78, 93, 109; assemblies, 10, 11, 13, 26; law, 10–21, 60, 68; legal tradition, 13, 26; orbis Romana, 108; religion, 112; senate, 10–11; soldier emperors, 15

Romanitas, 118

Rome, city of, 68

Rostovtzeff, M., 68, 70, 71, 110

Sacrifice, 21, 42, 43, 54, 56, 59, 69, 73, 74, 75, 76, 84, 101

Salpensa, 69

Salvation, 56, 84

Schism, 83, 92

Schultz, F., 12, 17, 20, 75

Schwartz, E., 9, 70

Scripture, 25, 93, 94, 104, 106, 111, 112, 119, 122; Paul, 45, 93, 102, 108

Sect, 68, 72, 81, 115, 117

Secularization, 116–17

Security, 8, 80, 110, 111, 112, 120

Seeck, O., 66

Setton, K.M., 65

Seviri augustales, 79

Sex, 7–8, 12, 21, 33, 37, 41, 43, 48, 60, 61, 67, 76, 83, 88–113, 123–25

Slaves, 43, 75, 76, 77, 99, 109, 111

Social classes, 60, 63, 64, 67, 68, 69, 72, 75, 76, 77, 87; curiales, 68, 69, 76, 77, 79; equestrian, 63, 70, 71, 85; episcopal, 67, 70, 74, 77; priestly, 67, 70, 77; senatorial, 63, 70, 71, 85

Spain, 12, 14, 34, 39, 54, 63, 66, 69, 75, 78, 80, 87, 110, 117; Christian, 4, 18, 19, 27, 28, 54, 81-84, 87, 100, 106; Roman, 9, 71, 78

Spiritualization, 105, 106, 112

Spontaneity, 11–14, 33, 44, 46, 49, 58, 112, 115

Steinwenter, A., 11

Strabo, 78

Suetonius, 61, 71

Sutherland, C.H.V., 71

Syncretism, 107–11

Tacitus, 61, 85

Tarragona, 63, 78

Tertullian, 36, 48, 60, 62, 77, 78, 82, 85, 93, 94, 96, 103–5, 107

Theology, 19, 25, 36, 45, 83, 84, 105, 107, 110, 112, 115, 117, 123

Thouvenot, R., 78, 79

Timgad, 15